Corners of the Mouth

A Celebration of Thirty Years at the Annual San Luis Obispo Poetry Festival

Edited by
KEVIN PATRICK SULLIVAN
PATTI SULLIVAN

CORNERS OF THE MOUTH
A CELEBRATION OF THIRTY YEARS
AT
THE ANNUAL SAN LUIS OBISPO
POETRY FESTIVAL

EDITED BY
KEVIN PATRICK SULLIVAN AND PATTI SULLIVAN

DeerTree Press
San Luis Obispo - October 2014

I want to thank my wife and Co-Editor, Patti Sullivan, for what you hold in your hands is a product of mostly her labors.

I want to thank Karl Kempton for his marvelous cover that makes my heart sing.

I want to thank Youssef Alaoui for his most generous book design, which also increases my joy.

© 2014 by Kevin Patrick Sullivan and Patti Sullivan
Front cover Art by Karl Kempton
www.thing.net/~grist/l&d/kaldron.htm
Book design by Youssef Alaoui Fdili
paperpressbooks.tumblr.com/store

ISBN 10: 0-9816119-2-3
ISBN 13: 978-0-9816119-2-1

DeerTree Press
1029 Southwood Dr. #N
San Luis Obispo, Ca 93401
(805) 547-1318
kpsslopoet@charter.net
kevinpatricksullivan.com
pattiartist@charter.net

www.languageofthesoul.org

This anthology is dedicated to my mother, Melvina V. Sullivan, to my father, Francis C. Sullivan, and to my sisters; Ann, Patty, Carol, and Rosemonda.

Thank you

Corners of the Mouth

TABLE OF CONTENTS

EDITORS' NOTES

Karl Kempton and I started the SLO Poetry Festival in 1984 and ran it together for the next 10 years. It has been my great pleasure to continue this marvelous event to the present. Over the years I have had much help from the local poetry community, the San Luis Obispo City Council, the SLO Literacy Council, the SLO County Arts Council, Cal Poly's WriterSpeak program, The San Luis Obispo Museum of Art and of course my wife, the artist/poet Patti Sullivan. This book is a celebration of poetry in the American tradition, bringing together some of the great voices of contemporary poets who have read here in San Luis Obispo over the last 30 years.

Our festival has always had the focus on readings. The voice of the poet with an audience to hear and listen to the words and images created with the language. To write the word and then say it aloud, to share it in a public setting, is a communal meal. We can all eat at this table.

It was with the help of Cal Poly's WriterSpeak, The California Arts Council and Poets & Writers, Inc., funded by The James Irvine Foundation, that over the years we could bring in Will Inman, Kathy Fagan, Carol Muske Dukes, Frances Mayes, Edward Field, Naomi Lazard, Denis Johnson and Eavan Boland to name just a few.

San Luis Obispo is blessed in I don't know how many ways truthfully, but one of them is the quality of poets who call the Central Coast home, from the Grand Lady of them all Glenna Luschei to the one and only "pops" Ray Clark Dickson. Between these two poles there is the Poetry God Michael Hannon, Kevin Clark, Dian Sousa, Gloria L. Velasquez, Nixson Borah and the new Poet Laureate for the County of San Luis Obispo, Marguerite Costigan, again to name just a few.

I'm really proud of what we have done here, not only with this book, but with the 30 years of the festival. It has enriched my life and the life of our community. That such a small town can have such a big ART/LIFE is a tribute to our imagination and the power of the spoken word. Thank you everybody, the poets who have read, the audience who has listened and everyone involved over the years.

Thank you – Thank you – Thank you.

Kevin Patrick Sullivan
Co-Founder/Curator/Editor
San Luis Obispo Poetry Festival/Corners of the Mouth

*

Where did the time go! I attended my first San Luis Obispo Poetry Festival in November 1998, meeting so many of the poets that I'm happy to say I can call friends today.

There have been so many opportunities to hear such diverse poets as, Ken Waldman, Alaska's Fiddling Poet pointing to an imaginary map with his bow; Larry Jaffe jumping up on a chair to expound from his "Unprotected Poetry;" the earth-shaking tremors felt as Merilene M. Murphy stalked the stage like Isadora Duncan; past Poet Laureate of California, Al Young enthralled us with his jazzy world; and Hernán Castellano-Girón let us peak into his surreal world.

What to say about Marguerite Costigan– I'll let her performance speak for itself when she reads at this year's festival.

I want to thank Anne Candelaria for inviting me to move up a little closer in the audience, to sit with all of them and later on for encouraging me in my own writing. I want to thank my husband Kevin for all his hard work, vision, commitment, love and for inviting me to be part of this world of poetry.

In the reading of these poems I'm reminded once again what a talented group of poets have graced the various venues at the SLO Poetry Festival. Of course, there would be no festival at all without an audience, so thank all of you for attending over the years and being such good listeners.

Patti Sullivan
Co-Editor

CORNERS OF THE MOUTH
A CELEBRATION OF THIRTY YEARS
AT
THE ANNUAL SAN LUIS OBISPO
POETRY FESTIVAL

Sylvia Alcon

LIKE WHALES, MAYBE

or dolphins,
from underwater my husband calls
a wheeze in rising waters
riptides pull at his lungs.
If he could hear the dolphins call,
he might find comfort in their song.
Beside him on the bed my breath joins
his, slow inhale, exhale, repeat.
I could go with him, breathe for him.
He gasps and grips steel bedrails,
quick, I grasp his hand, embrace
in currents that eddy between us,
and my feet brace
against the outgoing tide.
I listen,
and hear my own one breath.

Cynthia Anderson

NECESSITIES

A bevy of doves preen in the sun,
heads swiveling over backs and wings,
each bird slightly apart from the rest,
safe in a gathering spot among rocks.
The morning ritual comes after they search,
intent, for insects, pecking at crumbled earth
with the elaborate care of accountants, ledgers
duly balanced. Satisfied in their bodies,
they sit together in silence, absorbing
as much warmth as they can on a clear
winter day when human intrusions
are distant–the boom of live weapons fire
on the marine base twenty miles off.
The ground shakes after each explosion,
but the doves are used to it, unperturbed
by all but immediate threats to their lives,
their priorities in order, their foundation
secure until the day it all falls out
and away–which is not today,
impossible, not yet.

Roger Aplon

ELLIOT CARTER'S STRING QUARTETS No.4

First, there was the wind & the scent of Jasmine. Next, came the cat as cautious as ever & the bicycle-boy every afternoon at four. How much he missed her. Today would have been their tenth anniversary. From the corner of his eye he spied a flaw in the setting. Where was the table set for two, the waiters, roses, a chilled Cava? There was a ringing in his ear, a signal over the years, maybe mother again, maybe not. He'd swim out to the sloop. That would be the way. A mile maybe, not much more & a mile back. He hadn't tested himself in weeks. What better way to forget or was it *remember?* The water swallowed all those thoughts, it was icy to the touch, his fingers numbing with each stroke. The sloop had a bunk & a heater. Up the ladder & over the side. It felt good to be on board. To be on. To be. Once, in Barcelona, he'd hired a woman for the afternoon. She came & stayed for one hundred dollars. Her name was Doris, from the Dominican Republic. She knew what he liked & accommodated. Why think of her? Here? On board? Too tired to make the return. He thought of Tokyo & their meal of fried eel. Those were better days. She was there. In Rome they slept late, fucked in the morning & ate a succulent assortment of clams, muscles, shrimp & crayfish. By four the sun would be low but the wind might have died. He started back, the line from a rubber dingy between his teeth. His next trip will be easy. Maybe he'll ask Jaclean to join him. They'd make quite a pair, go to Ireland & visit her grandmother, drink lots of Guinness & visit Yeats' grave. What comes next is anyone's guess. Who can know? Who can ever know?

"As The Leaves Fall" – After: Elliott Carter's Five String Quartets

SHE WEARS A SCAR

She wears a scar that curves from her lip across her cheek to her ear.
She was cut by a man who found her home &

when she smiles (which is rare) it rises like another mouth &
puckers like it would open & speak &

when she runs (which is often) her features tense & her new mouth
glows like a wire – hot & powerful &

she wears one glass eye on a thong around her neck to see in the dark
&
a needle taped to her leg &

she flies a black flag with a man's face at its center & has etched
a red scar on its cheek & the number 6 between its eyes &

at the end of her street she's painted a door in the eight foot wall &
when she must, she opens it & runs through &

down the hill to the river & to the ship that carries her back
to the beginning.

Jasmine Marshall Armstrong

CALIFORNIA – LAMENT & FUGUE

California – you try to hide –
those half-moons of dirt, under nails.
A dark side moon reflecting our
long day's journey from
the fields, spent beheading
lettuce or delicately plucking of the grape
with the curved scimitar knife.

California, you want to flash us –
with pixelated sex, with bright pops
of flesh. You beacon us down
rabbit holes, into cartoon worlds
where we wield swords, rather than
cheap plastic phones, disposable –

With every passing season, with each
decimal point screaming that we
made it through the line, for the latest
juicy Apple, low hanging, before greedy
eyes, never thinking of the child,
in the Guangdong dormitory, hands

becoming bent at 20, like hands crippled
on this shore at 40, by the delicate, lover-like
ministrations to strawberry plants. More
fruit to be picked, to be dipped in rivers
of cocoa picked and pounded by another
child, in another continent, for our love's

fulfillment. This is Valentine's Day,
and California, the riverbeds do not run.
The bees have no blue white shooting stars,
those longed for blossoms, making an ordinary

cow pasture bust into song – the larks
are not here either. They've quit you and I –

I keep opening my throat wider, mouth
gaping, begging the sky to rent itself open
and give me water. Yesterday, the President –
suddenly gray as Moses, reed thin, a stalk
of last winter's grass, stood on this earth,
making the old call of Lent, too early –

Why has thou forsaken me?
there is no answer but this: In the hissing
of the BART trains, in the grinding brakes
of the freeways, in the idle cranes
of the port, in the wind raising poison
spores – the scream of eternal *why?*

Sara Backer

THE FOURTH NEST

To cut an old rose bush
into trash-can pieces hurts,
but the backhoe comes tomorrow
to carve blue lines on paper
into trenches in the ground.
To make a new dream happen,
you must give up the one you're living in.
So, I grab the shears.

Of course, the rose fights back,
slashes my sleeve, lops off a button.
A thorn burrows under my glove
and stabs a vein. Good shot:
I must stop to bleed awhile.
Then I see, in the dense center,
three strong canes that form a funnel
and in the vortex, in the thick of thorns,
are four nests, stacked on top of each other.
They're made of twigs, bits of dry grass,
even a strand of dental floss,
and lined with carpet fiber, matching
the carpet inside the house they lean against,
the house to be torn down.

What a bird!
Building a new nest four times over,
and in the same spot.
I think of all the miles I've flown
compared to this bird:
across the Atlantic six times,
across the Pacific twelve.
Massachusetts to California,

Alaska to Panama,
I've been there, been there, been there
and never done this before.
Never came back
to a town I once lived in,
the same jacaranda slapping purple
against adobe walls, the same brown hills,
like giant underground animals,
that breathe late at night
when the wind spins warm.

And I've wondered what I'm doing.
I still don't know.
But right now – bleeding –
tearing out the rose bush,
I'm grateful to a bird I've never seen
for showing me what can be created
out of instinct and patience,
and I salvage a stem with pink buds
and put it in a jar with water
to open up for you.

Dorothy Barresi

YOU'RE WELCOME

My dog delivers,
every day,
three petite piles
to the backyard

where it is my job
to recover, so to speak
them.

Sometimes fresh,
enough stink for a whole dissertation on stink,

sometimes crumbling white feathery excremental ash that is clean-
seeming. Fragile as everything
alive.

Usually segmented in threes: turd ellipses, turd SOS.

My shovel is awful.

Torque along its handle of splinters
beats a dull gong,
a reverb of infirmity in my future lower back
should I be lucky enough
to get there

We have art
so that we might not perish from the truth,

Nietsche says,
but it is pleasant enough
deshitting the green world
when I might be inside writing.

Sometimes I play a little game
with myself
How many piles can I pick up in one shovelful

before I unintentionally
seed the premises

with step-in-me.

Sometimes, at the precise moment I'm tossing
my dog's bad debts
her very worst drafts,

surreptitiously into the bushes that divide
my neighbors from me,

she'll look over her shoulder
and smile—

then squat down to new business

as if saying
You're welcome!
I know how you like to stay productive.

NO, NO—I'M HAPPY FOR YOU

Nose jobs are quaint. Poseidon has blue eyebrows. Good
      recessionistas
shopped in their closets—

I want to shop in other people's closets
Halos cost one pitchfork apiece

Are you one of those people
who's pretty in mirrors but ugly in pictures? Me, too!

Diamond dream-bra: coal pushed too far. 150 carats of heavy uplift
      open
your chest please to the Neiman Marcus

Firmament Collection. There's no offal in the offing
when cows eat grass, grass eats sun, and we eat everything, stop me.

My want-safe needs cracking.
When the bubble burst

I lost my bubble-wealth, matter and forfeiture, *fraise de bois*, substance,
accident, unicorns
purifying water with their luminous horns,

all of the all. Now worms cast
petite shit castles to bury us in. Mud frosting. Credit kicks. Moats I
      get:

you can always say – what, that? It's a reflecting pool.
My sleep isn't productive but my cough is.

According to the Egg Division of the California Ag. Ass., my heart
      may eat
two omega-enriched shells per week.

I don't want to bust anyone's chops, but there were rats
breeding all over the shell corporation I personally endorsed, alpha
      and omega.

People should care more about my problems—
I practice not saying that.

Will my soul, Tasered awake when I die, flicker daredevil and erudite
        like a bat
on dusk's soft current of mosquitoes

and late news setting forth, and eating as it goes, be satisfied?
Eat me. Pretty *and* dirty.

Three or four times a week I like to cast my bread on the water:
        Macy's, down-market Kohls,
my cast-offs go to the Rescue Mission

where mistakes live. The squeeze and the juice. Debt forgiveness:
like trying to lick your own tongue.

Who did I let down today?
That's just one of the prayers I say between

Please Don't, and *Now I Lay Me Down to Sheep.* Endlessly I stack names
        in dream's
container ships, then drift: Shove off, Mr. Creeper.

If the kingdom of God is within me,
He's got to be a little lonely.

Victoria Billings

MOTHER

We learned early on
not to ask if you were happy when you laughed
saw your smile
shimmer and disappear like mirages
over cracked asphalt
in the summer heat.

As children we crouched
among the geraniums and chives
in the English garden your hands planted,
waiting for smiles like rabbits
holding our breath when they came close,
afraid to break the spell.

We once ate all the parsley in the planter
shoved it in mouths
by the fistful until our stomachs ached.
We clutched at our round bellies,
moaned,
and you
scolded us
for eating all your carrots tops.

But at night,
when we lay side by side in bed
surrounded by toy beasties,
bears and lambs, you
told us stories of your childhood,
simple and soft
like parables:
of your mom in the hospital,
of your dad's first marriage,
of your grandfather saying
        "Honey,
            everybody gets the blues sometimes."

Laurel Ann Bogen

MEMO: A THOUSAND SINCERE APOLOGIES

We regret to inform
you that your life
    as you know it
has become irrelevant
and needs to be terminated

Please remember to keep
your arms and legs
inside the compartment
uniformly pressed.
Do not look to the left
nor under your seats.
Yes, you may breathe.

We apologize
that we've lied
    to you.
We are not accountable
for the failings of others.
But we apologize for them too.

THE MEETING OF TONGUES

Tongues whose lies sweeten lips like a sugar substitute.
Tongues with needles sew you to your crib.
Tongues of mayhem, tongues of deceit.
A probing tongue under a spotlight interrogates.
Tongues of lust, pink heart-warped desire.
Baby tongues, kitten tongues, imprint: they know not what they
      know.
The tongue of authority lumbers in the square, stamps yes stamps no
      with polished boots.
Tongues of the city size you up, chew, swallow, or spit you out like a
      wad of pale gum.
The tongues of lawyers clack with herringbone lips.
Some tongues, strategically placed, do maximum damage.
Some tongues are better left alone.

Nixson Borah

BACK FROM COLD COUNTRY

My heart leaped like a trout
when I saw fruit blossoms
in the front yard, after months
in cold country.

Stopping my car mid-driveway,
I walked close to the plum's
pearl-embroidered dress.
A few buds had burst open

in doll faces, porcelain
as my granddaughter's.
No hint appeared before I left,
and where I went,

winter lasts forever.
I came back leaden with grief,
bone-tired, unprepared for
these faces without shadows,

faint photographs punctuated
with dots for eyes and mouth.
True, the oaks are gnarled,
arthritic, lichen-flecked.

But flowering quince is ablaze.
Hoof-prints show deer
have danced in the iris bed,
frog song resounds.

Over long months, afterlife
was doubted, eternity dreaded.
Now this flash of the fragile,
then plunge of surrender.

Beverly Boyd

COMPASS

Averting his face from customers, the fair-haired
fellow restocked the market's dairy section, gave me
directions to the dried fruit, and pointed.

Before following his hand, I glimpsed a rimless
monocle wedged in surplus folds around his right
eye, then saw it was his only eye,

divined the absence of his left ear—
nowhere to hook a temple arm of spectacles;
he'd rejected a concealing patch.

The lens required no grimace, no apparent
strain. His single scope could surely magnify,
reduce, assess – foretell?   From years

of healing, his youthful skin had smoothed like desert
sand some parts of what he'd sacrificed for U.S.
claims, I guessed, on foreign oil. With what

he must have seen, his sight extended far
beyond the visions of those of us with double panes.
He labored behind the scenes, obliged to guide

yet another through unfamiliar terrain:
        You'll find raisins on Aisle 11.

Lynne Bronstein

THE MYSTIC CIRCLES OF YOUNG GIRLS

I'm finally having
A pajama party! Okay. Not like yours.
I've got only one friend over here, not six or seven.
But it's good to have one friend.
And no, my family has no party room in the basement.
We're in my room, on one side of the plastic
Divider and Anne's on the cot and I'm on my bed.
Anne saw Keith with another girl at the school dance.
Keith doesn't know Anne exists; it's such a bummer.
You said you watched a zombie movie and ate pizza.
Our yearnings will have to feed us.
I whisper to Anne and she giggles.
That makes me giggle too.
I know it is a tragedy that Keith doesn't love her.
But even if it is the tragedy of the age, we are giggling.
Did we wake my brother up, on the other side of the wall?
He's turned on the radio
To defy our noise.
Stevie Wonder has been invited to our party.
"Baby, everything is all right!
Uptight! Outasight!"
That just makes us
Giggle ourselves
To teenage death.

Ivan BrownOtter

INDIAN TIME

"You are a day and five hours late
for this interview" said the superintendent
at the Navajo school
"How come"

I looked at him and took a breath
as if to say Well shit Mr Superintendent
How did you expect me to find the place
There are no street signs
I'm not Superman
Global positioning hasn't arrived yet

Sandy roads curve in and out of rainbow clouds
circle back through red rock canyons
I can't tell an Indian road
from a sandstone pathway

I ended up in Lukachukai then Chilchinbeto
without knowing how I got there
I slept out in the middle of nowhere
under a gallery of glacial-blue stars

But I didn't say it out loud
Instead I said "I'm from Phoenix
You can't get here from there"

The superintendent laughed
"You're right about that
Several people applied for this position
but you're the only one who showed-up
You're our new English teacher
Looks like you're already on Indian time"

Christopher Buckley

SKY

My distinguishing marks
Are wonder and despair. —*Wislawa Szymborska*

What is it with the crows up there–
Complaining about us every day since
That first morning when, once the chemicals
Cooled and the color blue was decided upon,

We crawled out from under the sea
Raising our hands up with the hymn
Of oxygen? Space within space–
Like the sea. But there is nowhere

To grasp a blue bit of it, although
It's in my mind, clear and immeasurable
Despite night regularly rolling down
Its shutter and calling in the birds

Who sing because the thimbles
Of their lungs burn with the white
Idea of it, because it is the magnetic
Fabric of their minds, and leads them,

By the silver tide, home. Is it only
A wide opening to itself–the dis-
Associative atmosphere of the soul;
Where else does the incomplete sentence

Of the future end? No one in this thin
Caplet, at this faint edge, knows
Who's breathing outside the limits
Of our thought, which is to say

The universe is the way Aristarcus of Samos
Saw it one day looking out his window,
Eating a biscuit, when he was the first
To say the earth revolved about the sun

And it got him nowhere. So although
I look out via the interstellar photos
Into the original fires, where is it going
To get me when I want one more day

Of breathing along side the eucalyptus
And sage? Cave of air, all the estimations
Are flung up there and floating, like
Pollen, like shreds of cloud spread over

The horizon, the way my book reports
Flew out of my folder in 1959 as I raced
My bike down San Ysidro Road.   Since then,
Little has been clear. So far as I can see,

The trees are always unequal to the stars,
The Pacific coast is the edge of the world.
More each evening now, facing out to the light,
I feel the great blind motion behind the air.

LOOKING WEST FROM MONTECITO, LATE AFTERNOON

Beneath hills of agave and eucalyptus,
beneath the Spanish palms and walled estates,
I look across the bird refuge
to East Beach… mist in the channel
and only the outline
of the islands floating
vaguely on the blue, just above
the tide and spindrift
choruses of surf.

Half of everyone I've loved
is buried in the cemetery
on the cliff here,
or on the sea out there.
I remember the tangerine trees
just off the road
in Greenworth Place,
the overgrown bamboo—
we'd drop our bikes
in the high wild grass and
the clouds would trail us
until we turned home
with the dark

Now, I think
the gulls and white face coots
have as much of an inner life as I.
The clouds keep pressing.
I have been here 54 years –
I don't know
that I want to go
anywhere else.

George Burns

FORGIVENESS

Now, many years later, I stop the car.
Listen to the crinkly sounds of the engine cooling.
Watch the fog swell and dash
across the beach.

It licks at my windows and I am swallowed

I don't know what happened
Maybe there was a smell.
- He just jumped.
And my mother and her boyfriend,
in a fog of alcohol, drove on.

Could he have survived?
And did he stand on shaky legs
waiting for us to return?

Now in the distance,
the shaggy white surf
paws at the land.
I let all the windows down
and the night comes in

I start the car, drive slow.

Not looking in the back seat,
I can feel the night's
black nose,
cold and wet,
pushing against my neck.

Nicholas Campbell

ELEGY FOR THE LIVING
for Benjamin Saltman, d. 1999

"He'll live on in his poems," someone said
of my old friend who is dying, as if he were
already a ghost haunting his books instead
of a house. I thought of a poem most like him
in which he had become a house and said,
"When he's gone I'll knock down every wall
and not find him. Can someone who has
lived, live on in a thing and be truly alive?"
And then I read his poem.

He was there. I heard his voice say he was
a house that "does not want to move," as I've
wanted myself to say: If I could be a house
someone could enter after I'm gone I'd be there.
If he'll sleep when this book isn't read
I'll read it every day to wake him.
As I've heard of a child I know who tries to wake her
dog by pouring water on its grave.

"Cleo's in the grass," she told her mother
and then said, "That's okay, That's okay,
grass is everywhere." And didn't I hear
my old friend say this but in another way?
"Now I'm here but then I'll be everywhere."
So he'll likely be: I'll carry his book everywhere
with me. Maybe I'll hear one morning as I read
a poem of his without dread of him being
lost say: "Holding on is as good as flying."

Linda Camplese

JEFFREY'S NECK ROAD

Easy curve of asphalt, clean
stretch of road, between
downtown and Ipswich Bay
three straight miles no potholes along the way
to where moneyed folks moor their boats.

On the left, working Moms
with dirty kids, charm laundry from baskets to dry
like linen snakes, starched bed skirts fly,
new sails on ships aground, on the edge of town.

Marsh air perfumes quilts and sheets
eel grass waves and greets
monarchs and swallowtails
too many to count, a royal dance hails
in dust kicked up by passing trucks.

Running headlong, mesh nets fly
barefoot girls, pink, pale sky
catch winged jewels for lesser queens
golds and rubies and torn blue jeans,
by sundown wearing lilac crowns.

Anne Candelaria

AFTER SEEING THE TANGO LESSON
At the Palm Theater
(Remembering South America 50 years later)

How are the stars over Buenos Aires tonight?

Are the lovers doing the tango in the Copa del Rio?

And in the Cochebamba, old Bolivia,
is Oscar listening to Chopin,
the long steps to upstairs muffled and silent
in the dark?
More to the point, in old Bogota
is Alvaro alive? Alfredo, mi poeta?
Edmundo, my summer romance?
Fernando, my dancing partner till 3am?

El pasodoble, "El Relicario"
el bambuco,
the past now a shot in the dark
a door banging shut here and there
on "the roads not taken"

so that I could live this life here now,

eat this last summer peach

with its whisper of fall,

have this mellow son living three hours away,
that divorced husband, sober and a friend,
those smart students graduated, gone,
the dear mother blessed and buried-this poem
taking shape in the aftermath
drawing it together like a velvet pouch
full of jewels and polished stone
clinking the days, the weeks
and years against each other.

AND THE DAWN COMES UP LIKE THUNDER

For the gift of sitting in the early sun,
I give you thanks, Lord.

Morning comes with her wagon of surprises:
banjo music spilling over the fence
from a new neighbor, a climbing old rose
bush hiding the player,
an ocean breeze arriving unimpeded
through a space across the way
once filled by two magnolias.

Why did they cut them down,
I ask myself, but myself, as usual,
has too many questions
and so few answers.

What I can do is notice the path
of beauty opening up before me
each dawn.

I sit still.
Quiet as a nun.

CINCO BAYOU

Ft. Walton Beach, FL

Funny how one thing leads to another.
I am sipping strong coffee at a sidewalk
table in front of Big Sky Café, California,
watching the trees fill with sunshine
along Broad Street's red-brick buildings
when Zing! Like the pluck of a guitar string-
I'm on Cinco Bayou, my first visit
to Brother Jim and his Louisiana bride.

They stuff me with Jambalaya
and newly minted Key Lime pie
green as the slow water of the Gulf.
I'm so happy I'm ready to move into
one of the white-washed condos on the shore
but the alligators and insects under the humid
gibbous moon deter me.
My whole life shifts 180 degrees
on that sober decision. All that's important
happens afterwards: marriage, motherhood,
career, this poetry life.

Yet when the strains of Blue Bayou
come across the waves, I am back on Cinco Bayou,
Jim is still alive, moving his clumsy tall body
across a dance floor in unaccustomed grace,
Lorene a tiny drift of Southern honey in his arms,
one thing leading to another.

Hernán Castellano-Girón

CALIFORNIA

When we lived in California?
How long ago?
Two or three cats ago, it seems
Inside the darkness sobbing with me
The ones who lived with me up there.

How many times I lived my stories
Among the jazz aired by my brother Jim Cushing
Embracing the night like *Midnight Cowboy*
His music sounds in my ears fifteen years after:
If nobody knows the secret of the dead
Much less will know it we who still are alive.

All days in California were Mondays
But neither the moon set, Selene my sweet girlfriend.
All these nights brought the gift of the unknown
And the transparent.

Once on New Year's Eve night, a dance was offered to me
From then, nothing, all fields in California
Are filled with land mines
They have underground canned poisons since the SWW
But there were also some still alive seeing with my eyes
Kevin Patrick Sullivan, Don Wallis, Karl Kempton
All poets covered with morning dew
Early birds of earlier fallen stars.
Also it was Giuseppe the poet of ravioli
Friend of *Vieni Vai*, a restaurant where he imported its delicatessen
By airplane from Italy, there was no other way
To offer something tasting like from Lucillo's garden

Now who will drink your Marsala?
Who will taste your *profiterole*

And Sicily's *cannoli* filled of African perfumes and ricotta?
Who will recall you Gesualdo the Prince of madrigals
Who killed and died for love?

She by her side used to go to drink joining the fawns
In a creek springing Out of Nowhere.
There I used to sit in a trunk that once was a tree
Waiting patiently the one who would never arrive
Whose smooth legs were meant to be kissed millimeter by millimeter
From the little toe to the cracked watermelon
Which lies in the enchanted forest perfumed by musk

Now time has placed me a knife on my lips.
Time didn't want to give me its handout
Time is a Tequila Cuervo's empty bottle
Liquor good for crying like in the best of *corridos.*

Dolores you indeed were a Queen:
You ruled in a clean pigsty
With a young swineherd whom you still loved
Instead, he didn't love you any more:
He used to bed *igualadas* with onion's breath
You had to call the cops to send him back home
For just a week.

Now I can pronounce your name
Because my eyes will never look at you again.
In California they stayed, looking at the *Farolito*
Sung by Agustin Lara to coo the unfortunates
Of any time and place.

Now I can speak out
What is told by me steps on their way to the abyss.
Llorar, llorar y llorar.
In the midst of that chaos also the sweet Magdalenes cried
And Pluto the abductor was squirming of laugh.
I speak of women you never imagined
But you were going to mention once on writing.

When you speak from the threshold of death
Your tongue is free, your word
Also resembles a real slut
Who gives pussy even to dogs.

That was California: beaches without waves
And where they broke there wasn't any sea's smell.
On the pier of Santa Monica you sniffed a Dead Sea smell
And in others it was worse, because it smelled of lies.

An executioner walked on the sand
Where at the end of everything and also of the rails
Of a ghost train my Italian friend Lucia used to live
In a tiny house next to the dunes of Guadalupe.
A pelican kept her company on the roof of her cottage.
Everybody up there suffered hunger and thirst
Because they were satisfied
Three times satisfied in the three vertex of the individual:
Top sirloin, pancreas and thymus.

It's a shame that all are already dead
The ones who lived near me, and they so much cried
When I was rally leaving alone to the South, ignoring
That my heart had already left much time before.

I had writing paper but lacked of ideas
And when I had ideas I lacked the paper
Because ideas vanish as Klaus Kinski died
On a California beach next to a gorgeous naked black girl
Imagine KK and Antonio Preieto together in that Sergio Leone's
western
Really, they were two films making one
Like double look as one
In our imperfect remote vision.

The only perfection consists in to die
Like my cats died
Offering me their existence with generosity
Because they lived just for me not to die.

California is Mexico, and mariachis up there
Used to block my breath
But they could as well sing *Regálame esta noche*
On request of the subscriber, who was in a hurry, much hurry
To go to be shipwrecked in the South
Where always dwelled my spirit, Atman, Being.

There are no roads, they still aren't
Now that flesh has turned infertile land
What's written has rhubarb eyes
Blood injected eyes like those of the Prince of Darkness
Ears buried with my Toonces
Brother recovered from zodiac gnostic light
Despite I murdered him with flea poison
But don't worry my friend, I myself
Spread it with my nails on my whole body.
I am also loaded with poison tearing my guts
Like Nessus/Necius the Centaur.

I may forgive all, if forgiving exists
Boastful volatile measure or gag
I may forget all except the ones who gathered
In that treacherous hill with a mausoleum
With twenty rooms to receive friends
The true ones like doves and the false ones like Chinese dragons
Who ardently desired to celebrate our departure
Which never happened because our souls drowned in the Jacuzzis
Where the body bathed but also we drank
The Lethe's River waters, and the Terrible Black Tits*
Was singing like the young mermaids in the sea.
Murky river of Hell, draining drop after drop
Like the saline fluid instilling salvation
To better skin you in the days to come.

For now, away from California
New Years are old years, very old
To get a little tipsy we have to lick the glasses
Of the ones who have emptied them like thirsty wolves

And then crumble our bread, all the crumbs
Picked from the floor, which we were to eat in the future.

A future that now doesn't exist.

But let's trust the new moon, I say.

*The Terrible Black Tits: a character invented by Chilean poet Enrique Lihn (1929-1988) a close friend to the author.

Amy M. Clark

GOING BACK

Sometimes you have to go back
　　　for the thing you've forgotten
　　　　　　that you cannot do without-
　　　all that remains
of the food, or your notebook. So
　　　　you turn back, an act of subtraction,
　　　　　　hoping the thing is still there
　　　unimportant
to anyone but you. Your head is down
　　　You keep a horses pace: *I'm going*
　　　　　back, I hope it's there, back I go,
　　　have to, have to.
You pass the places you saw for the first time
　　　going forward, lusterless now, peripheral.
　　　　　　Usually, a person gets in the way.
　　　And years go by.
Somewhere – you know exactly where-
　　　you wait, hunched and quiet,
　　　　　a stone figure in a garden
　　　collecting rain.

Gail H. Clark (d.)

PIT STOP

The distance to Paso Robles decreases
with each turn of my car's radials.
I pull onto the rest stop off-ramp.
Inside the public restroom, I see
four–inch high letters scrawled
in red nail polish above the toilet tissue,
"For a good time, call Essie." On the wall
is a phone number. Urine permeates the air.
I wonder if Essie lives in Gonzales. Soledad?
Does she climb into truckbeds of the long haulers
who journey up and down Highway 101?

Every milage post I pass marks the longing
I feel to start over, to host another beginning.
Maybe Essie hitchhikes to a new future, rides
in a vintage Peterbilt, proclaims her innocence.
Essie drives my fantasy as I think of her as eager
to entertain. Unlike me, she may challenge
a veteran trucker as he rolls through the live oak
sprinkled foothills of the Santa Lucia Mountains,
to deliver on his weekly run to Gilroy, King City
and beyond.

Kevin Clark

"LE SECRET"
- *after Rodin*

I'd just stepped out of The Classical Tradition
When I saw her looking at the two marble-
White hands poised the instant before touching.
I hadn't noticed the column between them yet.
Her beauty was a given, but the discretion
In her gaze drew me like the dark avenues
Of her pleated print skirt. She'd tipped her head
To see something. The palm-high column at once
Joining and separating the right hands? Each one
Glowed near what it couldn't know.

How easy

To imagine those nights we'd lock together,
Sitting up, riding the pre-tremors
As candles flared shadows between us,
Our posture bolt straight as if emanating
From both of us at once, how we'd lift and drop,
Dive for the plummet promised in each iris,
How every finger anticipates the swoon
Beyond first touch.

She hadn't seen me.

She slid her weight from left hip to right,
Slowly circled the stand, her skirt circling
Before winding back. Could I be sure her gaze
Was a deep form into which I'd been invited?
When I stole up close to try the scent of her hair,
She didn't once turn her eyes from the hands, but
Slipped her fingers into the spaces between mine.
It was our twentieth anniversary. We'd come for art.

INDULGENCE AT MANASQUAN

Fifty years ago, my father handed me a kite string and I watched
The fluttering paper panels lift above this very spot.
Yesterday I mentioned the memory to my cousin Marilyn,
And she nodded in the acknowledgment of adult children
Bonded at fourteen by the precipitate deaths of both fathers.
What we almost say to each other, what we admit to
In our long-codified sighs is that even now we imagine them back
To life, standing beside us in the summer yard, near ninety, unsteady
On their feet, two brothers cackling in the old boyish manner, still
          prizing
Our silly youthful ways, even as they crack wise at us.

How can I take myself seriously when I'm this prone to reconvene
My father's breath and blood maybe two or three times a year
Though he'd been dead more than four decades? It's exactly the kind
Of indulgence I warn my own children about. Be truthful, I say.
The world as it is, I say. Not so fulsome it's false.

Near midnight and the air of the Jersey shore drapes my shoulders
Like a friendly arm. I don't yet need to turn back for the rented
          cottage
Where all the cousins' stories are saving the night. Maybe
It's true. Each one of us makes a myth of the soul we imagine ours.
So mythic we'll never vanish. If I reach down into the sand,
One hand digging blindly, no doubt I'll find a coin waiting all these
          years
For my grip, having been thrown from a pocket, its last owner
Once leaping with joy for a son who'd live forever.

FLASHBACK AT CASTELFRANCO

Dawn in Micanopy, Florida, and the old Impala
Floats the canopy roads, the last hours of acid
Stripping the protective film from the world
So every tree and fence blazes
With end-of-bandwidth jitters, my breath
A shallow tinnitus audible in the orbit
Of my limbs...I cut the radio and slow
To an idle beneath the live oaks, Spanish moss
Dripping to the roadside floor, my only god
The present moment. Then I turn off
The car lights to drift in new moon silence.
For a few seconds, a great maw encloses.
In beauty and terror, I flash the lights back on
To stay true to the road beneath the canopy,
And a white fence glows in a burst
Until I kill the beams again.
One fascination
And another,
The world's first question strobing on and off.

Thirty years later, on this moonless scotch broom hill
Above three sleeping late-Renaissance steeples,
All the little windows flicker on below
Like fireflies in the olive trees.
As the dark mountain hulks beneath the last bright shine
Of sky across the valley, the molecules
Of another air
Seem to flood this one. My ten-year-old
Stands with her binoculars and stares
Into the same alluring Tuscan spill, a silent vista
So redolent one can see how prayer erupts.
Aglow, entranced by sunset, she asks how far
To the mountains, there on the other side.
And as I answer in the explanatory lingua she loves,
A host of paternal lies rise, then resign

in my chest. For I know what she'll come to know
Some long, road-coarse night:
We live in two places at once.
There is darkness and there is the lit-up world.
And behind both
An immeasurable quiet.

Jeanette M. Clough

COLD

Alone, it has no shape.

When water rests, cold may take the shape of ice.
When a star blows apart, cold will inhabit its vacancy.

Outer space is cold taking a long rest.

The taste of cold is brittle.

Cold understands thaw and is mystified by fireflies.

Fireflies and angels overheat easily.
That's why they fan their wings.

There is a place for cold on my knick-knack shelf
among the porcelain angels.

When an angel breaks, cold enters heaven in a state of grace.

Angels, heaven, and grace may not exist.

Only space, the fireflies, and ice.

Lisa Coffman

NOT CHOOSING OTHERWISE

Here they say going to the snow. There we lay under it
as it came on. Without the trouble of choosing otherwise.
Let the heat of the rooms grow even oppressive
held within the generous, empty touch of cold
until we could bear a little of our own coolness,
stand naked in a room inside the snowing.
It limited our waywardness, as it did the tarry slide of rivers.
Muted the shapes of hills but retained them,
working as memory does, blessedly covering.
All day the slowness of it. The balked light.
A presence that would not spend itself in one impulse.
Or tears of the Virgin sent to anoint us
that cherished themselves on the way down and retained
remoteness even at the moment of blessing.
In my room under the roof, by the sleeping dog,
at my desk with a bird's nest brought in from summer,
and two horse bones that had worked their whiteness
out of the earth of the body
and then the earth where the body lay buried,
I typed small neat dark tracks on paper,
all of it open and slowly filling with snow.

BASS

Down where you are
nothing breaks:

not the heart
not the voice

and the pedigree crystal
gets to go on shivering
with what you put in her.

I admit I began listening
only after a grief
stilled and dropped me
down through the melody
and exposed your great timbers,
your mineral dark,
the fine seismic pluck of your canter.

So I came to love the mmmm buzzing my lips
more than the taste of the frosting.
I came to love the shake of laughter
more than the joke that went before.

You're the shadow required
for each thing that flies
except your shadow throbs back into body
and we're touching by the time I hear you.

Like the pelvis that carries
the chalky dishpile of the spine
you carry harmonies stacked above you

and that is why
the hips love you best
and sway as though your
notes opened within them.

Evelyn Cole

IN THE BAHAMAS

Tropical islands
have no need for
cathedrals

In the Bahamas
the ocean laps the shore
obscenely

Coconut trees
dangle vivid
yellow balls

White folks stroll
through green grounds
nibble club caviar
breathe silk air

Blacks comb green grounds
scrub club houses
thank God in square churches
for silk air

In the Bahamas
mosquitos go to heaven
where they bite
the hand of God

Marguerite Costigan

THE NOKOMIS FRITILLARY

If voice had wings, I think they would be these:
pale tapestries of smoke and ashes, rising
from Temple ruins left by the Saracens
and Christians both, after the spasms of war

or love. They would be these, flitting translucent
over dead mountain grasses and tough hillocks
of lichened stone, over the varied olives
and greys of frost-line trees with stunted limbs.

That *this* has wings, smoke-blue and charcoal-stained
on a pale background, leached of vivid color
as if by tears for the long fall of moments
stubbornly flowing out of reach – I think

the remnants of such leaching would be these
time-tattered patterns, following some path
unknown to mind-front, tracing the soul's shape
against the air, transient as any leaf.

If this thin page could leave a single print
on air, like that high-mountain butterfly,
I would not mourn one ember of this poem,
knowing its ash, like *that*, would wing away.

RESOLVE

In this forever landscape
of redrock and cedar,
sky wide as heartbreak,
riverbottom willows
more golden than sun-ball,

I must be something different
than what I brought with me,
this inadequate vessel
cracked and time-checkered,
I must be made over:

I must be something bigger
to swallow such beauty –
buttes melting downslope
in pastels and pebbles,
rocks tall as battlements
riven by lightening,
ridge upon ridgeline
ranging the horizon –

I must be something braver
than eagles and ravens,
I must be something harder
than canyons and hogbacks,
I must be something sharper
than reefs running tilted
horizon to horizon…

I must be something stronger
than iron or whetstone,
I must be something wilder
than coyotes and pumas,
I must be something purer
than the fire every evening

that creeps up the red slopes,
flame against cobalt,
cerulean, viridian,
till night puts it out again…

I must be something loyal
as the dawn that relights this
dawn after dawning,
the dark breathing out again
before breathing in.

JENNY'S CANYON

The dead they haunt us much as the living do:
spatter of laughter, a look back over the shoulder,
the scent of something passing through the room
and gone before lingering: of spices, petals,

or musk – a simple stirring of the air
that interrupts our thoughts. We try to call
it back, tug like a spider on her web-line –
but it is gone. Gone the way of everything

that ups and goes, in its own way and time:
leaving a room behind or leaving a life –
it's much the same: divorce, lost contact, ships
or airplanes that escape the radar-scopes,

runaways taking wrong turns, melting into
the streets – debris of entire civilizations
leaving no fossil record, no sneaker footprints…
Such is the way, Jenny, you must have gone,

winked out, a light bulb switched to off, a computer
crashed, even the prompt washed from the screen.
Yet you are here alive in this dead-end canyon:
a murmured wind-sound caught between the rocks,

a footfall on the sand, a sussurant echo
of choked-off laughter muted by your fingers,
knowing they mustn't give anything away…
You are here, Jenny, as you always were,

here in this old slot-canyon that's alive
with transcience, mirroring the labyrinth
of all our living brains – this redrock canyon
soon to be dust again, and laughing with you,

blowing like time-grains out across the barrens
that are never really barren of anything.

*(Jenny's Canyon in Snow Cyn. State Park, Utah, was named
after a child who died of leukemia. It was her favorite place.)*

James Cushing

LAKE TROUBADOUR

We meet tonight
by a shimmying waterline,
sleep in the open, like heels of a loaf.

Sea air cools the evening sand,
gulls rise into the cooling,
boys smoke and dream of things they cannot name.

The sultry dusks of their childhoods
cling to their beds
like unsigned documents

and a voice I remember returns,
keening and moaning
as the wind runs home.

The moon, pulling an all-nighter,
tugs at the sea, says
I want you all to myself tonight...

IN THE RARE MAP ROOM

The Atlantic itches,
the Pacific itches, all
the best oceans itch.
Let me zig
instead of making
dripless candles,
zag instead of
turning soil.
Tomorrow's a mule.
Despite my blameless
mumble I look
up from my laptop,
find no brothers,
no grapes. I grab at
a finger. What vein
of ore will love
my Irish belly, my
heavy boots, my fifty
year old overcoat?
My beloved rides a
laughing volcano and
brays to the moon.
She's got candy in her skirt.

THE FUTURE OF MIRRORS

Loving reason as I do, I asked my demon
to help gather angel eggs.
I acknowledged his ducks
floating on the creek that runs through town.
I wanted you but I saw only motes
of dust and a wrong-side-up map of heaven,
heard one angel howling in a ring of
silent ice-cream trucks. I loped
from corner to corner, prayer to prayer,
shielding my eyes in case a goddess
decided to bathe. If I had wings,
what fig-shaped figs and nut-shaped nuts
I would bring you from my nest!

Ray Clark Dickson

THE LAST WHALE

futtock shrouds of the topmast high seas
gray with distant flensing of bloodied bull whales,
aboard a half-brig, 372 gross ton, 183 foot two-decked
framed with white oak, chestnut planked with long leaf
pine
copper fastened and lost at sea in...

a twenty-two year-old kid who wanted to be...today
he would be a buff ecologist signed on as assistant
navigator,
young tar-scented gutsy lads, roaring sunburned
sons-of bitches
posing as words on Conrad's cold & boiling sea, yet
willing

in his soundless calm to breach the roaring forties
of the south latitudes
cosecant to polar distance to
cosine of the half sun

a barnswallow rests on the lazyjack,
310 miles S by E of Bermuda, a porpoise impaled
on a harpoon over the martingale stays
the girls back home like garupas in the water
legs spread for deep diving in the galley
of black-eyed skipjack blue-eyed
albacore dark-eyed blue-lined runner

waiting for a harpooned whale snuffed
to the loggerhead as neatly as an account exec
on the big street of dreams and
what's the difference in a wooden-hulled existence
without care for sea or storm

time to flex his wetsuit, grease lance,
mount the director's larboard boat
pull heavy oars of the board meeting

meeting to order sang the secretarial cooper's order
turning the stone on razor-whetted boarding knives,
wood to the blackskin! blows!

dead ahead! forty-barrel bull abound
this crucifying sea stoked with the hard bread,
water of Club 21

gray overcast strong winds chop the long
swells of cigar smoke as he waits anxiously
for a snick of sun
through lowering clouds of cologne
Miami tans varnished with bull spermaceti
beyond flickering cabin light of whale oil
burning lamps, to sea again
pulling the heavy share, watching a squadron
of bikinied squid bearing contractual documents, blowing
a drowsy sepia-inked screen
before the maggotswarm of sharks
gunning for his ambergris
carefully hidden in his secret belly
in the darkest part of him
but for the buglight lit....

the shouted song *Whiskey Johnny*
sung by the ring of bulls
as the larboard boat pounded, fell, rose
in the watch for weather

he adjusted his monkey belt and held the needle
overhead so they could see the color
of his pride in the morning rain
as the foresail goose-winged abanging
high on the swinging mast again

look sharp! raise a whale!
razor-whetted iron at half-cock for Johnson

far at the end of the table, forty-barrel
Johnson who opposed the merger, Johnson,
surfacing and blowing a vaporous nasal spray
of shredded invectives, swimming easily,
smoothly with speed, flukes barely
under the surface

in minutes the kill over the kill over
get over the kill so Johnson's widow
can play with his scrimshaw sperm whale teeth
incised lampblack designs, time

for his widow to bake a lonely pie
crimpin' the gunnel of freshly rolled piecrust
with Johnson's ivory jaggin' wheel, so now…

reach in the water and touch Johnson's crinkled
rubbery skin, touch the knobs, partitions,
to see what corporate life is like the instant
before death,

surfacing big bull he is O my God yes he breaks
water back from blowhole to hump
grease the lance take steady aim FIRE!

waifs and wigwags to the skipper

I've got Johnson!

toss out the barrel drogue let him swim
with the line in his bloodstained sea, *harpooned,*
waiting for the bloody boarding knives
to cleave his scarf of blubber, oil-tried-out and
casked for home.

THANK YOU VERY MUCH FOR THE LAST TIME

Kutaksia Vumeiseta
>   Finns do not thank each other
>   for a visit, but wait for
>   the next meeting.

Summer days without darkness; winter without light
but for the flare of her body
in firelight; raw/pine rooms, flax/covered chairs,
life brought back
to the 100/year/old bed.
Nakedness steaming in the log/fueled sauna; bodies
color of pink/fleshed salmon trout
found in Baltic inlets; her smell of birch leaves &
juniper berries; her aura, sisu,
a pack with pride & the past.
Toasting with frosted glasses of *kokenkorvo,*
a strong schnapps
biting the teeth of laughter with toasts of *Hei &*
Terveydeksi.

>   *to your health*

sharing broiled crayfish in dill with barley bread...

He felt, in dying; how that Cheater War
chose young salmon trout,
caught, sealed, gutted; smoked in the dull drone
of gunfire
fed with birch branches & bark shavings
in the round old oildrum of the world, lost in deep pillows
of arctic cloudberries, the hot & whirling whiteness of her arms...

THE LADY IN RED

As soon as my grief therapist
steps into her robe, skips out
       of my head
I return to the story that keeps
       me from drinking: be it pitiful
or apocryphal, it goes something
       like this—
A young American diplomat is posted
       to South America. He goes to five
consecutive embassy parties. At the
       fifth he sees a beguiling figure
in a red dress. He asks for a dance.
       The lady says NO for three reasons:
1) You are drunk; 2) They are playing
       the Brazilian National Anthem; and
3) I am the Archbishop of Chile.
       Then, thirst assuaged, I turn over,
go back to sleep
       counting the lambs of God.

Michaelann Dimitrijevich

MY FATHER'S SHOES

In Derbyshire
we walk up the torchlit drive
to a dinner at the castle.
This place is as old as fairy tales,
built with granite block
by unremembered men.
I touch the stones
and smell my father
whose craft brought him home
in crusty work boots.
He would sit at the yellow booth
in the kitchen with my mother
and sip a highball,
while the job of taking off his shoes
fell onto my brother, my sister or me.

When it was my turn,
I would sit at his feet
like a puppy
eager for him to notice me
as I popped the cemented laces
off the hooks at the ankle,
then pried them
through the holes at the foot.
The boots were hard to pull off,
they were such a part of him
and his sigh was always louder
than the one I would make
as I peeled off his hot socks.

With his dirt
on my hands

I would carry them
to the back porch.
They were heavy,
like the bricks
he laid that day for us.
For us,
so we could go to private schools
and orthodontists,
and riding lessons,
and have things he never had.
His shoes were heavy,
like the rocks
he would pile high
to make a waterfall,
like the stones
he stacked one by one
to build someone's home,
someone's castle.

Sharon Doubiago

LOVING HER AT LAST

My fifteen year old self, naked
walked into the room awhile ago
here on 64 Elgin Park, San Francisco

She just came in, moved around, then set on the edge of the bed,
the first time I'd seen her since back then.
I didn't move for fear she'd disappear
though she was so ominous
that seemed impossible

Eidolon, her breasts
were blue-veined beneath white marble.
I smelled her. I could have touched her blue-veined muscled thigh.
I was breathing inside her. I was
bleeding

I saw for the first time that she was beautiful.
She who had made me so miserable, a spectacle, a freak
her body   her thoughts   her heart   her presence
I've fled ever since

I had not realized my impoverished self, the state
of my soul until she walked into this room.
I had not realized how much I had aged
but in she walked, o my
in perfect preservation

just hiding all this time.
Moved around for my observation
as if she'd never left

> *(for Sharon Lura Edens, for all young women. Against the religions of Femicide)*

LYING MY EAR DOWN

"My tradition comes from the sounding of the sea, of sibilant language,"
— Jack Hirschman

Lying my ear down
on the crooked trickle of water
burbling through sand, listening to
the carving of canyon
Topanga

reading aloud your *Aur Sea*
curled on the two foot tidal bank
unreadable in the way I'm schooled
though familiar as from the heart of myself, the bible
of my soul (forbidden,
the language I know before words

were dammed, jammed back down my throat

The sun's rays on me, the hot sand
under me, Topanga gliding girl-like
into the pounding, roaring black-kelp churning sea, this book
Wallace Berman has brought me, you
sloshing through my mouth

Let me see a river enter the sea was my prayer as a girl
as we came down the mountains, crossed over the bridges, let me see
the ever-widening flow, splaying out gold
to enter the incoming waves. A river
entering the sea had to exist
but so rare in our developed desert
to glimpse such wonder
would be like seeing snow coming out of the sky.

Wallace is painting black alephs on boulders

in the creek up the canyon
and in the low tide line on the next beach north, rocks
under the waves, exposed once a month, lunar first letter
from the Kabbala
making sacred the land again
from the politics of art, from money, from the Holocaust
as you are making, too, *Aur Sea*

murmuring screaming sibilant song and menstrual too
the world in blood flow. Ravines to the rims, pure self
welling, wind and ocean currents slamming
the earth quaking, the grunion running
in deepest prayer

of non words, new words, shuttering old sighs, gasps, cries,
            stuttering, sputtering
dreams, ancient mouth of wagging Topanga tongues spouting
lost Chumash, found babble of my mother and gush of James Joyce

in loneliest longing for my own words, Ocean's
fear of what I might utter, my fear of what I will
say, throwing the sand back, blocking the flow, pooling
behind sealed lips

> she has no love
> no tongue, no blab, no words
> no Linga Sharira, no poetry
> that will carry her across, allow her
> to gurgle creek bubbles, milk words
> as you, privileged son can and are doing, so
> encouraged   so loved

> but your Topanga Creek father tongue
> is an opening, blabber and blubber
> at your mother's breast, suck
> of her story, for the mouth breaking open, creek of herself
> to the waves whispering *receive me, receive me...*

You who will never understand her love for you, you
who will always call her Marilyn. Did you know, revered Poet,
Monroe means mouth of the river? she lies upon

earside down
reading your poem into the sand
little Topanga trying to enter the Ocean
to enter the world
to become a poet

(for JAH, as he called himself when I first knew him: Jack Aaron Hirschman)

PRAYING MANTIS

(mantis, mantic: Greek for prophet)

Morning. The anniversary of my father's death. Suddenly
you are on my thigh. I scream
but you are weak. About three inches, your head
a giant eyeless green globe. I talk
to you. I get the jar, I get all the props, I talk
to you continuously. Outside the thirty open windows
through which you must have come, though who knows when, you
      must be
starving, grinders and generators and tractors and young men
making the asphalt drive to the new house obliterating everything
especially the smells, the grassy meadow, the trees, the sea
a quarter mile below. No wonder you're discombobulated
though the web site says the male praying mantis
cannot copulate with his head attached to his body.
To initiate sex the female rips it off. Have I been dreaming again
my head chopped off, Daddy, oh my prophet
preying on me still?

Now you're attached to the antique chair,
the left front leg, my leather jacket draped over the back.
Jar and lid still in hand I lift the whole thing, talking, singing,
praying, I love you I love you.
Together we move toward the front door.

You let me do this, you're getting ready
to lose your head. You let me put down oh so gently the chair
and open the big door, cursing I hadn't opened it first
before our precarious journey

and you let me pick you up again
let me free you to her somewhere out in the blazing sun
let me shake you off into the petunias
my daddy's large head, his widow's peak, O
mama amen

(for David and Carey Goheen, for The Sea Ranch)

Samuel H. Duarte

AGRICULTURAL LETTERS

I was raised in agricultural towns
wandering from one to the next
surrounded by a strange language
brought upon us by unstable winds.

I was raised pronouncing Spanish
double RR's, double LL's and silent 'H's,
while pruning, digging, pulling,
clipping and tearing roots
that have no place in this land.

In time, I was taught to
decipher the hieroglyphics
through repetitive incantations
untangling in dreams my
native language cradled on my tongue

I learned to fuse sounds into words
                         into sentences
                               into expressions.

I learned to curl my R's
smile to the 'I's
to the double EE's
and discovered that the 'H'
has a voice of its own
and that I could use it now to say things like
How Are You
Have a Good Day
I Hate Horseradish
Here is my Home
and Here I am.

Denise Duhamel

EXPIRED

When my mother says, *Take something of your father's to remember him by,*
I take his black and silver "D" cufflinks and an Albuterol inhaler—
the kind that comes in white plastic tube, the kind
they don't make any more. The code on my father's inhaler has

                                                        expired

but I don't care. My father put his lips to it
when he had trouble breathing. Albuterol didn't help
my father, but I knew it would help me
to put my mouth around it, to squeeze and breathe in something
he might have breathed himself. The inhalers they make now are

                                                        more

"eco-friendly," but the squirt of Proventil isn't as forceful.
I like the old Albuterol, but it contained chloroflurocarbons,
so the manufacturer stopped making it. I am all for the environment,

                                                of course,

since I'm asthmatic, yet these new inhalers in their yellow canisters
just don't have the oomph of the old ones. I am nostalgic,
just like my dad, who talked about the farm where he milked cows
in Canada. He never understood the appeal of skim milk
since that's what they used to give the pigs. He liked heavy cream
and whipped cream, too. Now everyone agrees
that skim milk is better for you than cream, that these new inhalers
are better than the old. The velocity of the puff is slower making it

                                                        easier

for the medicine to penetrate the lungs. At least that's what my
doctor says.
But I miss that blast in the throat, that fast relief, the way I miss

                                                        cream

when I'm trying to diet. The doctor tells me that honest, the

                                                medicine

in this new inhaler is the same, that it's just hard sometimes
to get used to change. I am using my dad's inhaler until it runs out,
until I absolutely have to say goodbye.

LITTLE ICARUSES

As I unscrew the dead
60 —watt bulb and shake
your bodies from the glass globe
into the trash, I feel
huge, like God
or science. As I screw in
the new sun, I blink,
descend, fold up
the stepladder. It's time
to paint on new lips
and drive out
into the risky neon mist.

WORST CASE SCENARIO

Your house washes away to sea. The whoosh is subliminal. You're terminal. It's totaled. They say you're a floozy. The trapeze comes loose. You're ten minutes late. He leaves you. He leaves you for someone else. He betrays you and begs you to stay. He dies. You dye it back to the original color. You move. You become a maven of rot. You sell the antique teapot. You can't stop the infection. He wins the election. Reconstructive surgery. You adopt. The child will adapt. You divorce. They use force. You get your cards replaced. Your mortgage balloons into a double bassoon. You start over. You overplay your hand. You wish you were dead. You get a new job. You steal food. Your bathtub crashes right through the moist floorboards and lands downstairs, demolishing your neighbor's bathroom. You move on. He won't let you take back what you said, no apology good enough. You use a voice-activated computer. You end up in prison. He ends up on parole. He makes his bail. You wear an eye patch to the mall. You try another brand. You up the dose. You take out the seams. Your trailer rooftop peels away like God is opening a can of Spam. Your insides get rained upon. Your haiku flops. You come in last place. You fall. You fail. You're too full to move. You look like a fool. You find out your winning was just a fluke. There's blood in your stool. Your car stalls at the light. Your mannerisms become stilted. You stand still. You become stale. You fall off your stilts. He slits his wrist. You make a fist. You get up too fast. You miss the feast. He foists himself on someone else. You end up in the state-run nursing home. You never grow up. Your hunger makes you queasy. You abandon your quest. They call you Quasimodo. You fail the quiz. You end up in showbiz. He kills your buzz. He becomes your boss. You go bust. You only make it to first base. Your blister pops. He calls the cops. You tip over your half-full cup. He flies the coop. His cap blows away. You get stuck in traffic trying to escape. You choke on a grape. You lose your grip. His hug becomes a grope. You get separated from the group. You stoop to his level. You don't see the stop sign. You trip on a step. You become a pest. You make a mess. The mouse is really a rat. The moose busts through the plate glass. They launch the missile while you sleep.

Jane Elsdon

LOOKING FOR A WRITERS GROUP

We returned from a long trip to an answering
machine surely exhausted by its endless blinking.

Among its many messages was one from
a vigorous sounding man named Charlie.

He had heard an announcement about our writers
group at a local book store on PBS;

Would I call him back to answer a few questions?
I dialed the number and a woman answered.

I explained I was responding to a message
from a fellow named Charlie who was looking

for a writers group. A cavernous silence followed
and what I thought was hysterical laughter.

My father has alzheimers, she stammered at last.
He wants to write a book, she blurted

before bursting into a storm of grieved sobbing.
Again a vast and hollow silence followed

while I groped within to compose myself.
You're in great pain, I babbled the obvious.

Yes, she responded. *I'm sorry.*
I understand, I answered, adding, *I'm sorry too.*

Sorrier that I could say, for a relentless fear
reverberated through me still from the evening before

when someone asked me where we had lived
before we moved here thirty-four years ago and for

an interval that felt like forever I could not remember.
I know why Charlie looks for a writers group.

I know why he is desperate to corral his words
between the covers of a book.

I know why he wants to tame them
so they can work for him again.

I know why his daughter weeps.

WINTER'S HARVEST

When winter comes
weighing us down
with weariness and loss
natural wisdom whispers
Lower yourself
into the lap of silence
where the shaman's song is born.
Allow her to cradle you
close to her heart
as soil cradles seeds
and roots softly hum.
You are thought
making its way into form.
You are fertility's gift
of rejuvenation,
the bearer of new life.
In the womb of silence
you are winter's harvest.

ONE MORE NATURE POEM

Your nature is quiet as high desert at dawn,
quiet as a wilderness trail twisting upward
to the remote sculpture of a Sierra summit.

Quiet is the air you breathe, the quality
of love in the room you inhabit.
It is the luxurious warmth and security

indivisible from your tall, lanky frame,
and our beloved peaceful presence.
Our home is silent without you.

Your recliner is overstuffed with silence,
an overpowering, raucous silence
rowdier than a Lakers game or ESPN.

It fills and permeates every room,
seeps into every crack and crevice,
It molds my moods, before it sweeps me up

into the welcome realization
how blessed I am, for your absence
is only temporary. Any moment now

you will walk through the door.

Clayton Eshleman

AT THE BRITISH MUSEUM, 11 APRIL 2007

That anything archaic exists today
attests to erasure's unbowed adversary.

How do I know this perforated antler from La Madeleine
    is alive?

Because, half-buried in it, a horse is emerging,
eyeholes filled with ochre,
a dream of ornamental blood.

How do I know I am alive?
Because, half-buried in me, my death is cross-legged on
   a cattail mat,
vertical carrion with illicit halo.
                      Sift
        of worlds
              open to
  faith in the sun lathe
around which the rasp of mortality is grating
a microscopic tundra scene.
         Leaf-thin
disc escape,   to wear it
              in my throat

for Pierre Joris and Nicole Peyrafitte

Landis Everson (d.)

DEATH IS A HOLE

Death is a hole, or a gap
in the hole. The radio talks Texan,
the plain outside is shabby.

A false desert lost in its own dream.
I think of the forsaken rabbits, hope
they come back to me. I was a sex slave

near Tecate in the Casa Grande Hotel
spread-legged on the dining room table
the man called me Mable

no rabbits were available. Insanity
not an option, was not a remedy anyway
but the song down the throat

of death did sound beautiful, like rain
over a dry place sucking for air as with
a knife in my teeth I descend the stair.

It was a border town called Gates of Hell.
You know it, too? Filled with rabbits that
forsake you when you need them the most.

They were bygone days that should not have come
on a phantom planet that death controlled
always around, damn it, like static on the radio.

THOUGHTS ON HANSEL AND GRETHEL
for Jack Spicer

The duck in the story who saved the kids
is you swimming through your poem,
the only hero in a bitter story
that everyone misses.

Your arms flail up and down
make the sound water makes when it talks
and the deeper you go
the words hurt.

But it's your poem
you swim alone in.
The fish accuse everything, rolling their eyes
the duck swims circles around blue skies.

The radio tossed in as trash long ago still
plays old love songs like new.
Air, water, love—
the vocabulary your words must breathe through.

Peter Everwine

RAIN

Toward evening, as the light failed
and the pear tree at my window darkened,
I put down my book and stood at the open door,
the first raindrops gusting in the eaves,
a smell of wet clay in the wind.
Sixty years ago, lying beside my father,
half asleep, on a bed of pine boughs as rain
drummed against our tent, I heard
for the first time a loon's sudden wail
drifting across that remote lake—
a loneliness like no other,
though what I heard as inconsolable
may have been only the sound of something
untamed and nameless
singing itself to the wilderness around it
and to us until we slept. And thinking of my father
and of good companions gone
into oblivion, I heard the steady sound of rain
and the soft lapping of water, and did not know
whether it was grief or joy or something other
that surged against my heart
and held me listening there so long and late.

AUBADE IN AUTUMN

This morning, from under the floorboards
of the room in which I write,
Lawrence the handyman is singing the blues
in a soft falsetto as he works, the words
unclear, though surely one of them is *love*,
lugging its shadow of sadness into song.
I don't want to think about sadness;
there's never a lack of it.
I want to sit quietly for a while
and listen to my father making
a joyful sound unto his mirror
as he shaves – slap of razor
against the strop, the familiar rasp of his voice
singing his favorite hymn, but faint now,
coming from so far back in time:
Oh, come to the church in the wildwood...
my father, who had no faith, but loved
how the long, ascending syllable of *wild*
echoed from the walls of celebration
as the morning opened around him...
as now it opens around me, the light shifting
in the leaf-fall of the pear tree and across
the bedraggled back-yard roses
that I have been careless of
but brighten the air, nevertheless.
Who am I, if not one who listens
for words to stir from the silences they keep?
Love is the ground note; we cannot do
without it or the sorrow of its changes.
Come to the wildwood , love,
Oh, to the wiiild wood as the morning deepens,
and from a branch in the cedar tree a small bird
quickens his song into the blue reaches of heaven --
hey sweetie sweetie hey.

LULLABY

Last night, in the dark, something
came near and frightened me
and left me turning in my bee, listening
to the hum of a mosquito—almost the timbre
of a human voice—as it came and went.
She must have entered from the garden
through the turn screen, looking
to calm a need of her own
and called to—so I've been told—
by the sound a heart makes.
No, this isn't another metaphor
meant to adorn a romantic tale.
Like you, I'd kill a mosquito in a moment.
But it does make one stop and think
how driven we are—even the least—to hear
the world's incessant undersong—
even if it was never meant for us
or never anything but clamor we wanted to be song—
and how much we love it, and with what sadness,
knowing we have to turn away
and enter the dark.

Paul Fericano

CURLY HOWARD MISREADS EDGAR ALLAN POE

The director yells *Cut!* and everyone on the set
is relieved to feel the weight of the day lifted
like a dark comedy of unscripted errors,
no one more thankful than Curly Howard
who retreats to his trailer for a quick smoke and a drink,
rubbing as he goes his shaved cue ball head,
where once the hair grew so thick
he actually appeared handsome to women
who fought to run their fingers through it.

He's reminded now of the sacrifices he's made,
the punishment he endures at the onscreen hands
of his older brother, Moe, who lovingly calls him Babe,
the mixed emotions he feels with each conk on the head,
each slap of the face or fingers poked in bewildered eyes,
and all the bricks and bottles and picks and shovels
and falling pianos and entire buildings collapsing
down around him in heaps of lowbrow humor and pain
can't hide the desperation of his clownish art,
the dreary midnight in his laughter.

Sitting alone, the alcohol convinces him otherwise
and he imagines himself a student of serious literature,
finding wisdom in the works of Edgar Allan Poe,
reading tales of unspeakable horrors befalling others,
grateful for this small refuge of scholarly insight,
and he commits to memory poems of young love dying,
mourning loss in a small room, much like this one,
childlike and powerless to rescue the slipping away,
the black doom of wings waiting above the door,
and he reads as he rocks, repeats the line
Quoth the raven, 'Nevermoe,' over and over again,
until he knows it to be absolutely true.

Adelle Foley

FOR MARY RUDGE

Came out of Texas
Scars of the great depression
Made you strong and sweet

You taught children art
Marched for peace and for justice
Traveled round the world

You published my poems
Taught me to work the camera
And roll the credits

At last we were stars.
Our 1990 feature
Is there on U tube

We'll miss those evenings driving
From San Francisco
To Alameda

Trading bits of news,
Plans, future projects, gossip
Riding in our car

Dancing in our dreams
You are forever our
Poet Laureate

Jack Foley

FOR EDWIN MASSEY JR: IN MEMORIAM

"In a theater full of empty seats, poets became their own favorite
audience…From 1850 to the early 20th century, from the post-Romantic
generation to the last Symbolists, writing meant exile."
—Ernest Sturm, introduction to Sartre's *Mallarme or the Poet of
Nothingness*

Age gets us all, Edwin
Even Southern gentlemen of
Impeccable accent
Even Southern gentlemen
Interested in history
As you were
Even Southern gentlemen
Of impeccable manners
"Jack," you would say,
"What do you think of…"
And we would speak of Life,
Meaningless, historical Life,
And if at times I thought
You flattered me,
I would expect no less
Of a massive, Southern man
With a magnificent mustache
And a gentleness
And elegance that belied
His massive frame.
You loved life
And thought
And were, I felt, of an accepting,
Philosophical
Frame of mind.
I can hear your gentle laughter.

But age gets us, Edwin,
Sweet man who bore
Much suffering.
History is the scrap heap
Of consciousness
And will allow us
Only a little fame—
If any.
You knew this,
And lived it,
Allowing your words
To touch the hearers
In those cafés
And shops
Where poets may be heard.
Your words
Touched me,
And I remember.
A sweet Southern cadence
In a Theater
Of Exiles

Michael C. Ford

SURF'S DOWN
After/Dian Sousa

Surf's down, surf's down!
It's like my beach, oh dude!

But the waves are all gnarly: I just
gotta get away from it, dude!

I really love all the girls from the
Osos Valley: the Vals are so grody:
they're really like rude!
But, please, stay off the sand at
Santa Monica Harbor: and what
makes you fer shur totally tubular
is like salt water's treated sewage
and the seagulls are all covered
with oil-spill crude!

Better to hang ten in the Morro Bay
pipeline: better to hang in the Hamlet
with Central Coast jazz; better to
chill in a fog-bound pass, better to
belong to Central Coast class.

IT'S QUIET ON THE CENTRAL COAST AGAIN

To IRIS in residual response

The Lompoc foggy bloom of tropical air
and moist currents shawl the coast way
below where you are in an, otherwise,
dry climatic region

In sunshine, in summer, even,
in the middle of cities, there's this
arid desert trough, where you consider it
to be low pressure Easterly waves

But, you witnessed another wasted sunny
bride with a temper like an Ohio tornado
and her voice jettisoning recollections of
a horizontal wind

Her hair was a jet-stream of cumulonimbus
clouds and another mother evolves into a
memorial bride looking over dense, vertical
imitations of matrimonial cliche' traditions

So just to keep it legal, as you listen to the
thunderstorms of family turmoil, too,
without forgetting the squall lines of divorce
where you envisioned isobars of arbitration

An equatorial fog mass hovers above love,
and there's no avoiding her occluded front
which will soon be forcing your father into
a contrivance of grooms.

Kate Gale

MEXICAN LIGHT

Went to Mexico. Curved sweet tequila light. Lay on blankets on the
beach, washed our mouths in the morning. Ate olives with sunshine.
Avocados. Street vendors sold popsicles. If someone had a hotel
room, we all showered. Our spectacular young bodies curved under
water. Our breasts moons. The room was white stone. We would start
with beer in the afternoon. Hit the cantinas in the evening. My friend
would find weed and Lily would breathlessly come back to my table
and say, Katie, I've found you a dyke, the cutest one in Mexico. We
would begin shots, chased with lime, tomato juice, the whole evening
a tremulous tequila bubble. They played our rock music in Spanish.
My boy would dance with me while Lily and I kissed the girls one
right after another. Mexico was like that. When I arrived blue, I
would find a blue world. Time moved the craziest of clocks.
Stretched on sand we waited for the end of loneliness. Night flies,
gulls and beyond them the sea. The sea spoke low sweet Spanish we
could almost understand. That was when I noticed what I liked best
about you was that you kissed like a girl, looked at me like a girl,
danced like a girl; the mescal was thick and smoky, your thin arms
came up around me as the sun rose. You said, I'll be whatever you
want me to be.

Dan Gerber

OFTEN I IMAGINE THE EARTH

Often I imagine the earth
through the eyes of the atoms we're made of—
atoms, peculiar
atoms everywhere—
no me, no you, no opinions,
no beginning, no middle, no end,
soaring together like those
ancient Chinese birds
hatched miraculously with only one wing,
helping each other fly home.

REFUGE

I watched the sunset on Mars,
through a space-probe camera's eye.

It dropped down so quickly–
like slow-motion film of a diver

plunging into darkness
through a last splash of light.

I heard soft knocking
at my door.

Then an acorn struck
and rolled forever down the roof.

A crow cawed faintly
beyond the closed window.

Autumn, and the fire
flaps like heavy canvas in the wind.

Sandra M. Gilbert

EARTHQUAKE WEATHER

Twenty years ago I'd have written
earthquake weather
a hard sun cracks the ground
the sea draws back

its nude anemones exposed,
and the great black claws of the cypresses
dig into the cliff
for dear life.

O all the phenomenal world
thickened with omens then:
the dead fish on the beach, the motherless
seal in the windbreak. . . .

And now—O now, dear life,
I tiptoe to the edge, peer over
the sliding foam that was,
the sticks and bones cast off,

while overhead a hawk
balances on a blue
hill of air, staring down
to where in the motionless

heat two bulldozers
flatten the next field.

MOVING OUT

Darling, I'm pushing the house
into the garden, into the black arms,
the green embrace
of the oaks. Yesterday,

two giants lugged the grand piano,
its synapses still crackling with your tunes,
up the steep steps, the narrow path
to the gate. Now it muses

in the *what is this* of a warehouse,
and the silence
where it used to stand
has forgotten to expect your *forte* laugh.

Out in back of the back,
workers dig in unsteady rock,
but now the house is moving
faster than they can hammer and hack,

the house has started to unpack:
its walls possess new places--
doors flap open,
windows heave off their hinges

and now the sofas are flying
into an amazement of ivy,
the hallways gaping
under a hollow of sky!

Only the piano keys,
hidden beneath their ebony hood,
remember your touch,
and wait, and are still,

and brood.

MARCH 13, 2004: SUNSET VIEW

At the first light of spring, I bring you narcissi,
their delicate pale heads drooping, drugged
with the breath of their own perfume.

How clear your stone is after all this time,
more than a decade since some unknown carver
was paid to drill your name in polished granite

and decades more since our youngest child was hurled
weeping into this same light of March.
Now your body that was once my body too

is nothing but a rag for spiders spinning
their own histories. What news do you have
for us? And what can we say to you that *means*?

Our youngest isn't happy. And the light of spring
casts an indifferent chill on the cut
narcissi that I flung across the stone

where your name still burns an eerie white
as if you could rise between its bars, above
the wilted flowers, the deepening marks that say

I lie among shadows with another man,
she lies alone with hope and dread. And you,
no longer you, you lie with the solemn spinning things

that move the light of March into its own decay.

–for *E. L. G.*

Valentina Gnup

THE CRIES OF ONE CROW

The cries of one crow can destroy a morning—
   somewhere in the world there is always a war.

At Arlington National Cemetery the headstones
   rise like white birch stumps in a ruined forest,

armed guards protect the Unknown Soldier,
   though what human does not go unknown?

In the National Liberation Museum in Groesbeek,
   a Dutch sculptor carves clay soldiers climbing

from their graves, smiling figures offer each other
   a hand. Cutting down a tree will not kill its roots.

One crow can torment an entire neighborhood—
   whose childhood is not scrabbled in violence,

each plastic grenade an education in war?
   The tally of the dead rises like snowmelt in a river,

I cannot unwrite their stories, unbury their graves.
   I can only hug the tall tree of my daughter, and

imagine the parents who wait for a soldier who will
   never come home. Somewhere in the world

a forest recovers, a stump is sprouting new growth—
   give one child a branch, he creates a weapon

give another child a branch, he raises his hands
   to conduct a symphony only he will hear.

Jaki Shelton Green

digging for grandmothers

"...the things that we love tell us what we are."
Thomas Merton

the house is quiet for sunday silent but for the usual visitation of the
    finches hovering
beyond the open window flirting with stray hummingbirds aroused
    by orange lantana
while prostrating fertile rosemary in pitch with flowering lavender
    engage in sunlit
foreplay interrupt holiness

never sweep your hair into the wind

i mistake my grandmother's voice for the sound of morning soft thin
    liquid like her hands
fertile iroquois hopi cherokee red hands that wrestle capture swallow
    hold light hostage
inside her belly teaching daughters granddaughters how to weave
    water into baskets

it is best to gather thunder on your knees

apprentice to wind and river forging centuries of breath into wet
    carolina clay
her pots jars bowls burial urns speak with swirling bear ribs turtle
    tracks wolf tongues
at my birthday she offered me to the water dervishes in hope of
    ransoming a wind she
could not name the house listens with me for the sound of
    crawling feathers

the disappearance of the somersaulting finches and paralysis of the
    air signal her arrival
i gather vials of jasmine sandalwood grabbing sage and cedar from
    the fireplace
reminding me that ascension requires aloe lavender amber white
    rose myrrh
this house sighs and remembers to breathe as I loosen long silver
    braids step outside

don't make a fist when you hold the fire's tail

my feet sing out loud against a selfish earth denying me the first
    embrace of red wings
beneath these crone soles roots grasses vines gather creating lush
    primal maps
kneeling beneath a canopy of iron and stone feathers where four
    generations of
hydrangeas bow ceremoniously i try to out sing the wind

ask permission of the plants before you cut them

i am your daughter harbinger to bone totems bottle trees moss
    mounds cypress arbors
islands of sea glass…teach me to dance across a ceiling of red

> *task of the daughter is to remember*
> *only your feet can teach you*
> *that the sound of earth opening in your ears*
> *will keep you walking upright*
> *the sensuality of dancing starts with the ear*

daughters of this dust

i

feeling real good
big boned
mahogany ass shelf
indigo left eye
same eye grandma found
rolling around in the cat's bowl
i teach geometry from unshaven armpits
geography begins between my toes
five different patois sing your name backwards.

ii

dawn colors my back mauve
you mistake it for argentina
shipwrecked soul
you pierce me with the knives of hunger
i cry a shark's song
for the loneliness at the bottom
of your eyes.

iii

your palms peel back my eyes
and stone the devils
living there.

iv

only you believed the blue eye
when she said she swam with mermaids
danced calypso beneath the sand
removed oshun curses.

v

feeling real good
impregnating condensed light
weaving new pigmentation
into right eye.

Jeanie Greensfelder

THE TRIP

I pack my suitcase,
each day adding more:
cloud blouses, sky skirts,
and a wind scarf carefully tucked
among trees and song sparrows.

Beside my daughter's buoyant spirit and her tears,
I position my son's pragmatism and heart.
I place Morning Man,
my rise and shine guy who adores me,
next to Evening Man who naps before bedtime.

I take Anne's listening, Coco's stories,
Terry's laugh and Eve's wonder.
At Costco, I toss in the little boy
sprawled on a couch,
and the old woman serving pita pieces.

And I'm in there at age four
bouncing on my parent's bed,
at twelve finding I could flirt,
at nineteen holding my baby,
at thirty-four launching a forty-year marriage.

I see myself in the mirror,
study the me I've become,
then peel my reflection,
fold it, lay it on top,
and close the suitcase.

Sam Hamill

OF CASCADIA

I came here nearly forty years ago,
broke and half broken, having chosen
the mud, the dirt road, alder pollen and
a hundred avenues of gray across the sky
to be my teachers and my muses.
I chose a temple made of words and made a vow.

I scratched a life in hardpan. If I cried
for mercy or cried out in delight,
it was because I was a man choosing
carefully his way and his words, growing
as slowly as the trunks of cedars
in the sunlit garden.

Let the ferns and the moss remember
all that I have lost or loved, for I carry
no regrets, no ambition to live it
all again. I can't make it better
than it's been or will be again
as the seasons turn and an old man's heart

turns nostalgic as he sips his wine alone.
I have lived in Cascadia, no paradise
nor any hell, but both at once and made,
as Elytis said, of the same material.
A poor poet, I studied war and love.
But Cascadia is what I'm *of*.

TRUE PEACE

Half broken on that smoky night,
hunched over sake in a serviceman's dive
somewhere in Naha, Okinawa,
nearly fifty years ago,

I read of the Saigon Buddhist monks
who stopped the traffic on a downtown thoroughfare
so their master, Thich Quang Dúc, could take up
the lotus posture in the middle of the street.
And they baptized him there with gas
and kerosene, and he struck a match
and burst into flame.

That was June, nineteen-sixty-three,
and I was twenty, a U.S. Marine.

The master did not move, did not squirm,
he did not scream
in pain as his body was consumed.

Neither child nor yet a man,
I wondered to my Okinawan friend,
what can it possibly mean
to make such a sacrifice, to give one's life
with such horror, but with dignity and conviction.
How can any man endure such pain
and never cry and never blink.

And my friend said simply, "Thich Quang Dúc
had achieved true peace."

And I knew that night true peace
for me would never come.
Not for me, Nirvana. This suffering world
is mine, mine to suffer in its grief.

Half a century later, I think
of Bô Tát Thich Quang Dúc,
revered as a bodhisattva now— his lifetime
building temples, teaching peace,
and of his death and the statement that it made.

Like Shelley's, his heart refused to burn,
even when they burned his ashes once again
in the crematorium— his generous heart
turned magically to stone.

What is true peace, I cannot know.
A hundred wars have come and gone
as I've grown old. I bear their burdens in my bones.
Mine's the heart that burns
today, mine the thirst, the hunger in the soul.

Old master, old teacher,
what is it that I've learned?

Michael Hannon

SWEET SPRINGS

Under a raw and limitless winter sky,
bright minnows mark the clear freshet
where it penetrates the sea, and is ruined.

A roosting hawk, not frightened by aging bipeds,
lets us wander close enough to see a dragonfly—
isinglass wings crushed between talon and bough.

Memorial benches line the path
that leads to the bird watching station where
life's dream, worn thin, allows glimpses of the void.

A windy day then—
the heart neither this nor that, the light in the trees
splintered against the day moon's giant face.

AUTUMNAL

In my trouble when my trouble was new,
a song was constant in my orphaned head.

It was the flowers, secure in their fiery heaven of roots,
singing the sun to earth, and brushing it with pollen.

Over time, that song became the sky's blanched patina,
her clouds bruised from being knocked-about and lied to.

Now, on a picture-perfect lake, countless shallow waves—
the old row-boat, blue once, tugs at its rope.

My trouble and its song, a joke in the turtle's throat.

CONTRARY

Giant blond hills, miles of dead grasses
sticky with thistles, and snowy mountains
hazy on the blue horizon not to be believed.

Everywhere I look there are traces
of botched and failed husbandry—
tumbled fences, ruined hutches, stray dogs.

I feel a benediction, a profound stillness.
My brain is making a vision of the muse asleep,
abandoned in her heaven of motes.

A voice in the light is humming
ain't gonna study poetry no more,
and I delight in the squandered paradise.

Ginger Hendrix

MATCHSTICK LOVE

My husband says to me: *Maybe we should remarry*
if one of us ever falls into a vegetative coma.
I don't hesitate– "You can do what you want,
but if I wake up and find you with somebody else,
I'll kill her and then break your legs." He laughs hard
when I say this, thinks my baseness is funny.
I could consider working on this trait, but I've got
other things to do, more pressing personal growth needs.
I think that if he didn't laugh,
Id fear for our love. I'd have to wonder
what had happened to us. He refuses to believe
in the worst of me, sees it as a veneer, I think–
a protective coating that has to flare–like the beginning
of a match stick. That if he laughs while the first bright
flash goes by, he'll get to the real flame.

Angela Hoxsey

SECRET COWGIRL

I thought I wanted a teaching credential,
But what I really wanted
Was a concealed weapons permit.
I thought I wanted a six-figure income,
But what I really wanted
Was a heart-shaped ass dipped in denim
Cinched in by leather and silver.
I thought I wanted a Ph.D.,
But what I really wanted
Was a four-wheel drive pick-up
And a gooseneck horse trailer.
I thought I wanted a marketing executive
With a walk-in wine cellar
Full of French labels
He could pronounce perfectly.
But what I really wanted
Was a crack shot with eagle eyesight
Who shoes his own horses
But still throws back more
Burgandy than Budweiser.

Kenneth F. Hunter (d.)
11/22/1963 ~ 5/12/2001

ALL FLY HOME

There was a song I used to sing to myself
when I was feeling sad or small
but the years and the tears have worked their magic
so that I forgot the words and all
but sometimes when I see a bird flying
and it stirs something in my heart
the song begins a slow return
or at least I can recall this part

    Sing child sing
sing with all your might
don't fret about a thing
it will surely be alright
    Sing child sing
sing with your own sweet song
we will all soon get our wings
        God's children
        All fly home

Like a child who opens up her hand
and the balloon tied to a string
flies to some far off land
and no one can explain a thing

    All fly home
home is where we want to be
where the cold world can't get in
home is where they hug your neck
        And whisper
   "Where have you been?"
"We missed you, where have you been?"

Will Inman (d.)

meanings i must almost
leave my body

the nearly round eye of the mantis
stares across sky tonight
bright with pearl from deep places

sharp claws of star-reaches rake my ribs—
dark blood and blue night swirl—
my feet lift from earth, kicking—

nobody ever told me coyote howls
sound the sharp of pain down, in...
i only heard distance without the spines

o cactus, cactus, how bitter you are,
caught in my throat like last words
of a dying god, don't say my name!

the damned leave footprints in our blood,
their paces teach us lost lessons—
what hermit crab! what desert!

o thorntree, how sweet you sound,
silence haloes every sharpened stem,
what tongues are impaled in your fierce wisdom?

i water you every dawn with my rage
i water you every dusk with my despair
i water you at midnight with my hope
i water you at noon with my laughter

you thrive whether i water you or not
your roots are fastened under my ribs
your leaves are the beard of a she-god

your voice speaks meanings i must almost
leave my body to hear, but i contain you – o
i'm shredded to dry jerky by all these things

nourish yourself well, this flesh is healing

the argument

i'm arguing with the rainbow

Why don't you curve in a straight line?
Why don't you build a square
                              instead of a semi-circle?

As well argue with a hill,
answers Rainbow,
as well argue with a river

You're nothing but broken-down light!
i contend, taking a different line

How beautiful are my wounds!
cries Rainbow, then whispers,
How wise, my crippledness!

No such a thing, i argue,
It takes a storm to bring you out,
takes the rage of wind to evoke you

What a healing storm, murmurs Rainbow,
what compassionate rage

You have no humility! i accuse

True, says Rainbow, *my curve*
is of the lips of god

An upside-down smile, i observe,
triumphant

Only to one who is upside down,
smiles Rainbow

You expect me to stand on my head?
i protest

Just see me with your ribs
whispers Rainbow

old chinese song

Why should I waste my time
in cemeteries? All those ancestors thrive
ready, in the potter's wheel whirling
from my skull to my ribcage, shaping me
out of themselves and against themselves

yet the world is a walking
mausoleum, and i can't bury myself
away from it all in mere
meditation.

Oh, I sat in the lotus center
with my root into darkest mud
until sun fertilized me
with hot fat pollen, but then
a bee stung me, and I cried out,
for I was on his territory
where sun and water and flower and mud
are ready to be doubled ever
in the six sides of his honeycomb.

Yet the queen bee heard my cry
and came out of the hive to me;
she showed me how to make honey, and
how in every hexagon cell of the hive
sleeps in amber the soul of an ancestor
of hers and mine.

She gave me some of the honey,
and it was like eating the singing
of many joyous and sad people.

My tongue increased in wisdom.

That is why I shall not tell you the rest
and also why I do not waste my time
in cemeteries.

Larry Jaffe

SOLACE OF AN ARCHED EYEBROW

Your eyes –

Do they remember
running
chased
and herded
onto ghettos
quarantined
isolated

You tell me –
The word ghetto
was born in Italy
where Jews were
restricted
to the island
of Gheto,
forever forced
to live
on reservations
of their discontent

They were –

15th Century commuters
walking
across water
to mind
their own
businesses
in the inner city

[I am] locked in
holocaust
memories,
living
my own
personal ghetto.

Your eyebrows arch as you look at me –

I find solace
just beneath
the arch
of your left eyebrow
framing
a perfect eye
that looks deep

Will Jones

HOW TO EAT CACTUS APPLES

From my experience, I recommend
eating them with your imagination.
Do not, while walking the trail alone
succumb to the allure
of the ripe fallen fruit
gathered in a fertile mound
at the foot of the cactus.
Do not, in childlike innocence,
bend down and pick up the reddest fruit
with the seemingly smooth skin.
Do not peel the skin back with your thumbs.
Do not raise the fruit to your nose
and inhale its exotic tropical fragrance.
Do not plunge your index finger and thumb
into the juicy golden flesh and extract
a shimmering morsel of sweetness.
Do not place the shimmering morsel of sweetness
in your mouth and swish it around
like newly poured wine.

If you do not do these things,
You will not find your tongue and palette
studded like a bed of nails
with countless microscopic cactus quills.
You will not find yourself spending the rest
of your hike around Paradise Mountain
plucking and spitting like a man with
a mouthful of loose tobacco.

You will not find yourself
distracted from the moment
and the glories of the hike

by composing in your head
a poem about how to eat cactus apples
hoping you won't forget your best ideas
before you get home and put them all on paper.

David Kann

LETTER TO L. COHEN
April 3, 2009

I skulked out of poetry's house at thirty-three.
At sixty-three I returned like a sneak-thief
because time could terrify me to staring silence.
And one April Shabat night you,
you seventy-five-year-old mensch, you,
you blissed out 7000 people for three hours, you,
with a nothing voice, a so-so growl, and a true voice isn't always or
            often pretty,
wearing a narrow-brimmed, slouched fedora and a gangster's suit and
words that showed me that time is no more than a limp dick,
words that stiffen my arms and legs with bones of diamond and
            teach me that what I thought I knew of hours and days is as
                                                                        nothing
to one word following another, certain as a path finding its way
            through a stubbled field,
sure as a night stream carving rock under a winter moon and
            gas-blue snow,
knowing now that years are no more than rocks knotted on a rope
            dangling in a still pool.
I pull them out one by one, each one another benediction.
The rope disappears in the pool, is slimy with algae, may slip away
            with the stones' weight, may fray and part

but I heave the heft and haul of years into my palms, hold each one
            in hand for its moment, sing to each cold rock, cradle it until
            it warms and breathes

Sincerely,

D. Kann

Rachel Kann

DAIYENU

had you –i been given but seconds in this unreal reality,
and the ten-thousand things not made themselves known to me-you,
daiyenu,
had the ten-thousand things made themselves known to me-you,
and your-my blood not thudded circuitously, stubbornly,
daiyenu,
had your-my blood thudded circuitously, stubbornly,
and these atoms not stayed gathered into matter as me-you,
daiyenu,
had these atoms stayed gathered into matter as me-you,
and you-i not been born earthly entity,
daiyenu,
had you-i been born earthly entity,
and these lungs not breathed me-you,
daiyenu,
had these lungs breathed me-you,
and you-i not strengthened from struggling,
daiyenu,
had you-i strengthened from struggling,
and the time-space web not caught me-you,
daiyenu,
had the time-space web caught me-you,
and you-i not made manifest believed-in possibility
daiyenu,
had you- i made manifest believed-in possibility,
and never felt faith inside me-you,
daiyenu,
had you-i felt faith inside me-you,
and not lost ego-identity,
daiyenu,
had you-i lost ego identity,

and not detached from a conceptually separate me-you,
daiyenu
had you-i detached from a conceptually separate me-you,
and never found inner tranquility,
daiyenu,
had you – i found inner tranquility,
and never let angel-death tongue-kiss me-you,
daiyenu,
had you – i let angel-death tongue-kiss me-you,
daiyenu,
had you- i answered with reciprocity,
and not still vibrated energy for eternity,
had you – I been given but seconds in this unreal reality,
had it all been arbitrary,
had it all been but a word,
a breath,
a blink,
a touch,
a grace,
a pulse,
a truth,
daiyenu,
daiyenu,
daiyenu.

Nicholas Karavatos

PASSPORT CONTROL: PARANORMAL AT THE BORDER

Little people native to America ruled by archangels

He may cause to be
But Guy Ballard was not the first George Washington
And he won't be the last

Seeing Findhorn twice
Before finding my caduceus

Survive the psychic attack
Of hag syndrome
With hallucinogens

Light crowns the head

It is an odd universal life force
That Colonel Henry Steel Olcott chants
While driving his Diamond Vehicle
Through the Upanishads

Like the Dalai Lama
But not him
Neither acupressure nor acupuncture is a course in miracles

Smoking medicine in the sacred pipe gifted by
White Buffalo Calf Maiden
Perusing an out of print encyclopedia of elemental thoughtforms

That which is received! God's throne-chariot! Undated book of
        creation!

Attributed book of splendor! Four walls without end! Divine influx!

The Avebury henge predates the Druids burying the Bronze Age
Backward drift of vernal equinox
The Great Conjunction was one month before the Ides of March

It is a vision quest and I am alone
My avatar, The Grand Ultimate First, is not online, is
Outside of cause and effect but connected in principle

I am a phantom of myself having
A near-life experience

Karl Kempton

OF INK
for Karl Young

1. A

As the first letter
was made like a pyramid
tomb of alphabet birth

2. 4 i's

Inkwell sun behind horizon
the scribe of dusk
dips the quill
to dot night's i

Venus

≈≈≈≈

The desire
to dot the i of air

from which
they

as birds
would become

dinosaurs invent
the feather

≈≈≈≈

The i has been cast
head floats above body

What we have become
the vanishing points
the planet falls through

≈≈≈≈

By holding the e handle of ode
Crow dips the o
in the soapy water of Gnosis
and blows the bubble he flies into
as the dot that completes Nothing

3. The Third Eye

Himalayan yogi saints
to complete the perfect
continental cursive i's
float from mountain top to mountain top
diacritic diadem bindu beacons

4. The others

Of the slingshots
u more difficult
to hold than y
pulling diacritic ammo

5. A calligraphy

Night's calligrapher
sharpens his quills
in the solar wind

the meteor lines

≈≈≈≈

Standing on Venus
feather with crescent moon hat

Writing with sunlight

≈≈≈≈

Laying lines on ocean at night
the planets sing of sun light

SILENCE IS YOUR NAME

MATH OF NOTHING

math of nothing

mindless x ( ) = less mind

nowhere x( ) = now here

$$1\div \quad = \textbf{0}\text{ta}$$

Klipschutz

WILD WILD WAYS

Don't mention the old days.
You're talking to yourself again.

Somewhere between the bar and the café
you got lost at sea and drowned
in your tears on the sunken dance floor
in the spinning light the storm-watch night,
as the band went overboard, over a face
that is the absolute harbor of desire,
featureless, irresistible,
end of song.

You're talking to the girl you used to be.
Saying what you needed to hear.

Steve Kowit

I STAND IN THE DOORWAY

Sometimes when you say goodbye you know it's goodbye for keeps.
You touch your lips to her cheek, or you squeeze his hand & walk off.
What else can you do? Out on the street, the light has never
been so intense, luminous, intolerably bright.
But mostly we don't know when it's that last hug, the final goodbye.
Who would have thought that perfectly casual "Hey, Steve, take care,"
was the last. Years later someone mentions that Greg's living
somewhere in Spain or Rebecca got married in Quito. Don,
someone says, is in Shreveport. Or you hear through the grapevine
that Kenny has died, someone you once loved, someone with whom
you spent endless hours laughing back in those feverish days
on that other coast, in that other life. One morning you turn
the page of the *Union-Trib* & among the obits there's a picture of
     Larry,
from the old coalition, & you read that small notice beneath it
your heart stopped dead in its tracks. One afternoon,
at Dennis's bookshop up on Girard some guy you don't quite
     remember
starts shaking your hand & tells you that Susan died of stomach
cancer five years ago now. "I wasn't sure that you knew." & in fact
you didn't know. & Eliot Burke, swallowed by time. Was that the last
goodbye, there in the narrow hallway of that 6th floor walk-up of
     mine,
all those decades ago? Eliot grinning that edgy, cherubic grin &
     turning
to leave, & me with my hand on the tarnished knob of that door
     watching
him make his way down the stairs in the dusty, fluorescent semi-dark
of that place fifty years back, that door which hasn't yet quite shut for
     good.

NOTICE

This evening, the sturdy Levis
I wore every day for over a year
& which seemed to the end
in perfect condition,
suddenly tore.
How or why I don't know,
but there it was: a big rip at the crotch.
A month ago my friend Nick
walked off a racquetball court,
showered,
got into his street clothes,
& halfway home collapsed & died.
Take heed you who read this
& drop to your knees now & again
like the poet Christopher Smart
& kiss the earth & be joyful
& make much of your time
& be kindly to everyone,
even to those who do not deserve it.
For although you may not believe
it will happen,
you too will one day be gone.
I, whose Levis ripped at the crotch
for no reason,
assure you that such is the case.
Pass it on.

THE BLUE DRESS

When I grab big Eddie, the gopher drops from his teeth,
& bolts for the closet, vanishing
into a clutter of shoes & valises & vacuum attachments
& endless crates of miscellaneous rubbish.
Grumbling & cursing, carton by carton,
I lug everything out:
that mountain of hopeless detritus—until,
with no place to hide, he breaks
for the other side of the room, & I have him at last,
trapped in a corner, tiny & trembling.
I lower the plastic freezer bowl over his head &
                                        Boom!—
slam the thing down.
                        "Got him!" I yell out,
slipping a folder under the edge for a lid.
But when I open the front door, it's teeming,
a rain so fierce it drives me back into the house,
& before I can wriggle into my sneakers,
Mary, impatient, has grabbed the contraption
out of my hands & run off into the yard with it, barefoot.
She's wearing that blue house dress.
I know just where she's headed: that big
mossy boulder down by the oleanders
across from the shed,
& I know what she'll do when she gets there—hunker
down, slip off the folder,
let the thing slide to the ground
while she speaks to it softly, whispers
encouraging, comforting things.
Only after the gopher takes a few tentative steps,
dazed, not comprehending how he got back
to his own world, then tries to run off,
will she know how he's fared: if he's wounded,
or stunned, or okay—depraved ravisher
of our gladiolus & roses, but neighbor & kin nonetheless.

Big Eddie meows at my feet while I stand
by the window over the sink, watching
her run back thru the rain,
full of good news. Triumphant. Laughing. Wind
lashing the trees. It's hard to fathom
how gorgeous she looks, running like that
through the storm: that blue
sheath of a dress aglow in the smoky haze—
that luminous blue dress pasted by rain to her hips.
I stand at the window, grinning, amazed
at my own undeserved luck—
at a life that I still, when I think of it, hardly believe.

Richard J. Krejsa

FROM MARS TO MEADOW ROAD

Rain sprinkles predicted by Maine Public Radio
and Channel 6 weathermen have passed,
cloud cover obediently disappears.

West Wind whistles through giant Blue Spruce
rustles leaves on three Aspens that guard the
horizon of Art Wunder's 120 back acres.

Milky Way above seems close enough to bite
as arc of Southern Sky is illuminated by
butterscotch glow of the Red Planet.

Coy dogs howl in the marsh beyond but only
the cricket chorus, computing in Julie's garden,
can digitize the miles from Mars to Meadow Road.

Robert Krut

OUR JOURNEY WILL BE TREACHEROUS

You can carry the world's largest garbage bag
full of fingernail clippings across the country
only to have it traded out for a car-sized ball of lint,
which you must push back up and over the mountains,
like the great and dusty Sisyphus of the Rockies.

One day, even these tragedies
will seem mundane.

In my satchel, a museum:
postcard in a ziplock,
a dog's tooth on a string,
and a map with a hand-drawn giant
drinking the Great Lakes.

A long dormant volcano bursts
from the ground of an anonymous downtown,
launching the luncheonette sign to the heavens,
wraps its lava tongue around the corner
to peel my skull of everything but
one eye and a mouth.

One day, I will even
look back fondly on the moment
I discovered my fingerprints
blown against the side of an abandoned post office.

I remove the postcard from its casing,
hold it to my vantage point and see
its painted, majestic stallion midstride.
The handwriting on its back smudges,
translating the message into a new language.

Through the city streets, a hundred horses
gallop along the pavement, rush past,
lift the card to air, and head straight out of town,

only to return after racing the face of the Earth,
losing many along the way.

Tom Law (d.)

BOTTICELLI'S ANGEL

To Reinette,* my wife

You sought to be this work,
To haunt this vivid mirror,
To stick the slip of time
And splatter stops of black and chrome
In a frame of mind.

I will paint you lying on your side
Eyes closed, holding a ghost.
I will paint you lying on your back,
Eyes wide open, heels locked about life.
I will paint you with an eyelash for a brush
On the silver canvas on the moon.
On your knees I will paint you
With your hands around a butterfly,
Monarch and mate, tongue and thigh,
I will paint you standing straight
Where your shadows fill the spaces
Spread between the shrinking sparks
Over the toothed texture of the awful truth.

When I am done, sketched the last dark line,
I will scrape the palette clean again
And you and I shall hang it high
On the western wall of the world.

* *Reinette: little queen, French diminutive*

Benjamin Daniel Lawless

IDES OF MARCH

So Julius Caesar was speeding down I-15
on the way to Vegas
and he's texting his girl
and he's all like "Cleopatra, baby. Hit me back, girl." Send.

He's dancing between lanes,
dodging cars and couches that drop off pickups,
when his cell beeps.
Cleo: "I can't believe you forgot about tomorrow!"
Jules: "Baby, I'm gettin' you a great birthday present. Don't worry."
Cleo: "It's not my birthday, you oaf!
I'm not texting you back till you remember what March 15th is."
Jules: "Cleopatra! Don't do this to me. I love you baby."
Jules: "Hello?"

Just about this time, Julius Caesar has got this all-consuming need
for a rest stop. One too many Red Bulls.
So he pulls over to a gas station, does his business,
and on his way back to his Chrysler 300
he sees his good friend Sam Clemens
next to a car filling it up.

"Jules!" Sam says, "I am so glad to see you! My car broke down.
I managed to pull in here, and I've been pretending to pump gas
for the last three hours, trying to figure out what the hell I'm
        gonna do."

Julius laughed. Twain was always doing this kind of stupid crap.

"I'm headed to Vegas, man. You want a ride?"
"Hell yes," said Sam. "I thought you'd never ask."

They get on the road, but Julius can't stop checking his phone.
"What's going on?" asks Sam.

"Cleopatra's busting my balls, man.
Says I'm supposed to know what tomorrow is."

"Your anniversary?" asks Sam, laughing.
"You better wise up son.
March fifteenth will be the death of you!"

Lance Lee

GREAT UNHAPPINESS GREAT JOY

Coyote cries carry down a wind
    that adds a wolf howl from the eaves:
night falls on woods late heat burned
    then storm stripped, so autumn is
betrayed into winter before winter.

Against the long, Atlantic dunes
    waves stutter with mounting anger
while wet snow piles heavily inland
    and breaks leaf and wire then boughs
to sheet the roads with debris,

a night Lear tears at the sea-walls
    or ranges the moors and woods
that shake with his rage and fear
    his bare hands, spume-soaked beard,
his howls the wind's...

Would there was a blank place on a map
    labeled 'World's End', a place known
only by warm rivers that flow from a
    heartland where we imagine
no tremble in the light reminds us

of wings and a sword brandished
    to bar return, where neither
the world nor innocence is marred.
    Instead as this heavy-handed
nor'easter thumps to come in

we savor cranberry muffins
    fresh-buttered from the oven

that melt on our tongues —
    and debate what latest cruelty
we have done each other

to plumb again the well of forgiveness
    that lets our lives go on, common,
human, at times humane,
    without recourse to the greatness
only great unhappiness calls forth.

On the morrow as the storm recedes
    we survey its ruin, near blind
from the clear light, and think soon
    amid holiday cheer we will mark
birth in the death of the year,

while at twilight when leaf and limb
    release some of the light they took in
so each glows in its own hue,
    just then, for one moment, despite all,
we too feel lit from within.

WESTON WOODS

How green the dark in Weston woods –
    if you look for me here in after years
I will not be haunted, or haunting,
    but imbued in a seam of bark or a rustle
of leaves or the heft of a stone from a long,
        low wall –
    and if you sense my stare, turn quickly –
we will be face to face. In these woods
    the years are leaves that never fall
but flutter around me so time so irreversibly
        one plus one
    runs every way down these paths, splits,
        circles,
            rejoins,
all entangled:
                the car I gun up an icy hill
        into a tree;
    a woman a girl mine who melts beneath me
as the Sound licks the shore and sighs roll
        off the swells;
    my father who slaps me after a graduation
        all-nighter;
my daughter who steps on a copperhead
    too lazy to turn and bite – she is three,
        and death sleeps:
and me, who time out of mind strains for
    sense in these woods.
Fireflies begin to light the dusk. Here
    they are on and off at once, like ourselves,
        at once dark
            and blazing.

Eleanor Lerman

A WAVE CAN BE A PARTICLE

Here is the problem: that the life the body
contains may not be the same as the life
that the mind imagines. Indeed, the suspicion grows
as time expands that we are hiding things
from ourselves. Big things, shaped like nebulae
or chandeliers; in other forms they express velocity
They are going so fast that we doubt we saw them,
but we did. Before and after we were born, we did

We do. Which is why the suspicion grows that
laid out on a cold bed in the dying light may be
the fate only of bones. That there is, perhaps,
another example to consider: as a wave can be
a particle and a particle a wave, you need not
chain yourself to the belief that a steady state
is the singularity that holds all value

but may think, instead, of the feeling that
comes over you in the moment before a
weeping ghost appears to you (and only you?)
from the darkness beyond the bedroom door,
or approach the threshold you must cross when
you go into the woods and find yourself upon
the hidden path that, rumor has it, leads directly

into the void—but step, instead, into
another springtime. On the flowering lawn,
a girl you swear that you once knew
is laughing, and all around her (but not
only her), the windy sky is full of stars

WE HAVE OUR DOGS AND THEIR ANCESTRAL BLESSING

If tomorrow,
it turns out that our lives
are more mysterious than we thought
but our connection to each other deeper,

involving secrets about the creation of fire
and the folds of time that figure, mathematically,
into the distance between our encampment
and the distant stars, then even so

we believe that we are ready
More ready, probably, because we are friends
The scouts say it is dark up ahead
but we know how to live from meal to meal

We have our flags
We have our dogs and their ancestral blessing
Out on the road, we will survive the winter
In the spring, the wind will write its thoughts
upon the future

It thinks of us
It thinks that we will win

WHAT YOU ARE ENTITLED TO

Where are you traveling? Supposedly, wherever
your ticket says, though all you can remember
of your movements in times gone by is that
there was some vague appointment to be kept
in a distant city. Perhaps, if it was a sunny day,
there was a place where you would have stopped
        to eat lunch

But where are you going now? There was a plan,
once, to seek out Ilion—do you remember?
To ingest whatever was being sold in the markets
and slap the faces of those flat-faced, marble beauties,
the ancients who would not answer us. Who conceived
their revenge in the shape of beasts and whirlpools
Obviously, darlings, they knew things
        that we do not

So why are you packing? Who told you
that you have to go? Instead, you should ask
who enslaved you, who tied you to the years
and broke them like rocks into hours and
days and abandoned them on your doorstep?
Who made the rules? Who threw stars at you
and lied about their power to beat inside you
like a heart? Your heart beats on; it is written.
        It is known.

Then why give in? Remember that even the sight
of a train leaving the station diminishes as the
observer watches it depart. He or she (your choice)
will soon forget you; he or she will ply their trade
with others who are supposedly more desirable
Therefore, your job now is to loosen your grip
on the observer; the time of comings and goings
        is almost past

All that is left is to fight your way into the
great hall of invisible forces and tear up the timetables
Time tables. See how easily they split apart? If so,
then you may simply choose to turn them. If so,
then marble hands will applaud you and all the seasons
will send you messages from the future, which you are
entitled to read where and when you want to,
      one by one by one

Paula C. Lowe

JAMIE HERE I AM/TOE HOLD/DUST

I am absent in the house
of catastrophes to come,
the house boarded up
before or after the cyclone,
the dust storm, the rise
of the tide into the second floor.

I am absent in the way that lips
leave lips, skin flaking into wind.

– Jamie asks where I've gone,
asks scrub trees and small listeners.

Say, I am in the lineup on Easter Island,
I am in the crushed stone under asphalt
on a road to the south, to the ever hopeful
but ever bleak south.

Say too, I am an afterthought
rinsed out of cheese cloth
from a time of milk and cows and grass,
a thought to cry, oh, stop sucking on the tits

of this planet, you empires who refuse to grow up:
inside bassinettes, playing with thin screen gadgets,
playing with buttons instead of toes.

– And that is it, Jamie, who can keep a reason
for toes when no one counts on them?

The man who lost everything steals
something from his neighbor.

The girl who lost her virginity
searches for it on her knees.

– And that it is, Jamie, each village on the edge
of the earth has too few hands to keep bodies
from leaving their people.

Suzanne Lummis

EVERYWHERE I GO THERE I AM

No self-pitying poems.
— Caroline Kizer

Two women lean at the cafeteria
counter in the last great
dime store downtown, Broadway

off Sixth. They've journeyed
through aisles of shower caps,
dollar jewelry, baby toys,

just to sit down. The old one's
hair's gone pale, tied back
like a trickle of snow,

her limbs so thin she could be
lifted on strings
like a puppet, then let go.

But her friend had looks—she maybe
followed her star, came West.
Now she nightshifts someplace

for her bus fare and low rent.
She thinks, I bet, *to hell with it*
and rubs out her cigarette. *Some star.*

Yeah, it all adds up to one long
ride down
the escalator to the bins

of cheap stuff where you settle

for what you can get, then back up
for some lukewarm tea.

Don't be fooled, it's just
another half-disguised
poem about me.

Check back in twenty years
or so, you'll see.

LAST REPORTS FROM THE GONDOLA
SUSPENDED BY BALLOONS

> "Three months ago a Japanese
> piano tuner attempted to float
> over the ocean in a gondola
> suspended by balloons and has
> not been seen since."
> *The Los Angeles Times*, 1993

Laborers, tax payers, husbands
to unfulfilled wives, wives to workhorses
of middle management, you bearers
of just-bearable burdens, appointment keepers
and risers-on-time, good citizens loyal
to the Emperor, friends,
look! In all the world there's just one
Japanese piano tuner gazing down
on the Pacific from a gondola
held up by balloons. I am the last
possibility that has not been exhausted.

The climate is fine, cool sunlight up here
where my loneliness rings
like a tuning fork, and a slow stream
on the Persimmon Wind keeps me
wandering forward through the sky-colored air.
I feel like an illustration in a children's book.
Mother, when you held me wrapped
in butterfly prints did you ever dream?

Uh oh, friends, the evidence
of the gauges and my own eyes tell me
I'm starting to slip.

Could it be my plan needed fine-tuning?

This raindrop means a storm
gathers up there and down below
the sea will get even deeper.
Despite my quick adjustments
I'm losing height.
You know the feeling – like trying
to hang on to a great dream or wake
from a bad one. I wish that pane of water
were a window I'd sail through but
it's not. It's filled with sailors and still
hungry, still thirsty.

Colleagues, brothers of the guild, remind me:
in the findings of Wertheim, what
are the velocities of sound through pine,
oak, birch, through ash?
Through a *solution of common salt?*

I had a dumb and beautiful idea—
hard enough, isn't it, to stay aloft
even on a smart and homely one.

In the sky or on earth, now just one technician
plays upon this exact terror touched by wonder.
Still, I can't help but think of a new joke –
for the Americans, it's funny
in English: that crazy tuner went up, up,
till he was lost in the high C's.

Salary men, servant women, bosses
who answer to bosses, friends, I did this
for you – you who won't recall just where or
who you were, when my decaying aircraft
became my declining boat:

Uncharted Desire,
a vibration, a question, a hung note.

Glenna Luschei

COMINGS AND GOINGS

In Tucson
when a university student
goes home
she might leave her desk
and a chair, a book-
case outside her cave
with a sign, "Take me."

And who could resist
heat radiating over furniture
like a mirage? You hoist
an old Victrola into your pick up
and ratchet up a new song.

You start that life in the West,
invent a past, and when that tune
winds down, it's okay to put out,
"Take me."

What do we have in life
but comings and goings.

WATERMELONS

Now you watermelons
when thieves come
pretend that you are frogs
—Basho

While our boys fought in France, braceros came North to work
the fields. When mother heard they had only a cot
she took sheets and blankets to their camp.

A man she knew pulled his wagon along our street.
"*Sandías, sandías,*" he called.   Mother spoke
to him in Spanish. One oblong watermelon looked like a submarine.

We could see U-boats plowing up the Missouri. Men built
a tower in my Iowa neighborhood to spot the zeros from Japan.
My father was the air-raid warden and climbed the tower

when the sirens blew. We lay scared in bed until he called,
"All clear, all clear," so we could turn on the light.

"El corazón," the bracero said and plunged his machete deep
into the heart of the submarine melon. He speared the most
delicious dripping wedge I have ever tasted in my life

or ever will taste.
I could spit out the seeds.

"Say *gracías,*" said mother and gave him the quarter he asked
for the melon.

Later when I moved my own family to Albuquerque, their
          neighborhood
was different from mine: Vietnam protests in the street. Our first
          night
someone stole Erich's bike.

Sunset, we drove into the red, red heart of the Sandia Mountains.
No watermelons in Sandia Pueblo. "Green reed place" was their
ancient
name, a good thing in the desert. We bought watermelon from
Safeway.

BLUE ARROWS

Albuquerque: up early to meet the milkman
with his four quarts for my children, cottage
cheese and yoghurt for me.

We moved here from a country with sun moist
as the round Colombian cheese
wrapped in a banana leaf.

In Albuquerque the sky is shooting blue
arrows. The milkman tells me he prays
to the petroglyphs as he walks the Galisteo

Labyrinth, oldest in the new world. He says, "I rev
up the gods and they rev me up.
It's a two-way street."

The milkman my only friend in a new town,
my mother comes to visit. When we take her
to the top of Sandia Peak.

She passes out. We discover her low
blood pressure in her days at Lovelace Hospital
"I liked the Western art," she says.

A year later she is well and we go to the State
Fair. Now we have friends. I buy a pot
from Harold Littlebird. He gives me his poem.

My daughter Linda wins a blue ribbon for her painting
and poem. "I am the bicycle. I come along
to brighten the way. I ride away

leaving everybody happy." They all made me
happy: the milkman, my mother, Harold Littlebird,
Linda. They all rode away.

Amy MacLennan

RITUAL

Top sheet first,
tugged up to pillows,
goose-downed, mashed,
and they're next in line
for plumping and placing,
our heads just here,
my pillow sideways,
yours still with a curl
of my hair coiled
into the threads.
The comforter now
with two or three shakes,
cotton on cotton,
fibers frictioned
across each other
one last time.
And now the bed waits
like I wait
to unbuild our bed again,
strip it apart,
toss it into a mess
of longing and night.

Tamara Madison

DROP DEAD!

You spat it out like venom
at your playground enemy
and it felt so good to say
Drop dead! Late in life

it becomes a sweet mercy
to imagine: one minute
you're treading the earth
as ever, the next you're gone!

No hospitals, MRIs, CAT scans,
surgery, no loved ones
standing around wondering
if you're still breathing

and what to do with you
in case you are. And though
I'll never be ready for you to go,
as long as it is your wish

to leave this way, it is mine.
And may it happen on a day
when you are singing with friends,
laughing at a joke, dancing

in your living room.
May it come to you before
you know it and you'll find
yourself flying, a balloon

cut loose, taking one last glance
at this fond world that you have loved.

Though it will feel so cold to us,
this world without you, still

with all my heart here is my wish
for you dear friend, mother,
kindred soul: when the time comes,
Drop dead!

Maía

TRANSLATIONS

Winter Solstice, 2013

Light turned around this morning— bees in December
don't need a savior, translate nectar of marigolds

into red honey to feed their queen, their sisters.
Shooks and glints articulate the palm fronds,

the fingers of my hand, writing, the neighbor's green
striped curtain —*breathing* .   My love who died

beckons me closer. Shows me he is Artemis
wearing the skin of a deer, *I translate*

immobility into flight, the arrows of that melody
sing along a pentatonic scale, black keys

on the piano, holes in the barrel of a Native flute.
Starlings and sparrows translate air

into time running faster, swooping backwards
until I'm a newborn

resting in a young woman's arms—
she stands on the porch, naming me for carolers

joy to the world, though it's war
darkening the eye of the globe.

Marigolds this morning, the red taste of honey,
the sea's erotic restlessness— Earth, I tell you this

so that when I die you will translate my body
into palm fronds, my voice into bees.

Adrianne Marcus (d.)

LA BONNE AVENTURE (Painting, 1939)
The Good Adventure

> *Defying Gravity*
> *"The Invisible Cannot Be Hidden From Our Eyes…*
>
> *All that Counts Is The Image."*
> – Rene Magritte

In Chagall, the Rabbi floats; the bride and groom linked
Effortlessly in the night sky. Two days after you left us,
A woman stopped me and asked if that were a mountain
Lion running the hills behind our house. I knew that she
Had seen what we could not. Now you are here, not here.
Invisible. We are left with our imperfect images.
The sky turns into the Magritte Hour, lamplight warms the three
Windows facing the street. Nothing but clouds remain,
As if the storm has passed and the sky will clear by morning.
Winter's early darkness arrives. Down the hill, porches and eaves
Cascade with white icicle lights staving off the short days.
Something that resembles joy has come to visit. It defies gravity,
The persistence of sorrows, and says, there is love still
In this imperfect world, bright moments beyond
Pain. As I light the menorah, this, the last day of
Chanukah, I think how these eight candles bridge
All the centuries of darkness and how, repeating what
We call light, light comes.

Jacqueline Marcus

THE BLACK APPALOOSA

At dawn, I watched the black appaloosa from the upstairs window
Walk from one end of the lake's shore to the other.
He's old now, and maybe this is the equivalent
Of some daily prayer belonging only to the solitary silence of horses.
I don't know why my heart was aching with the ache of the living,
Or why I could no longer summon the language that carried me over
        the waters,
That made the light through the rain the only sound of cold.
I look out to the hungry fields, to that distant farm up the hill lined
        with cypress
As if it were a sanctuary, a place to rest my head against the sky,
A place of resignation where it just doesn't matter any more.
This moment too will pass, but such moments are filling up the page
With a certain kind of autumnal darkness,
Something that we secretly deny and prepare for in the end.
The sun is spinning through the bare branches of the pines,
The rain-soaked leaves of November are shining brightly
Like bronze-colored stones at the bottom of a stream.
You can fool yourself for a while with the fame and fortune,
And the stories you repeat for good measure, a little sugar, a dash of
        salt,
The small and insignificant pleasures that made you happy,
You can take it all and strap it like a bundle on the back of the horse
And you can go with him—any time now—to the other side of the
        shore.

Edward T. Martin

THE BARRACKS GAME

My first day home from war, at supper time,
My father startled me by asking at once
About my medals, "What were they given for?"
My smile was modest and confused.

My mother interrupted, "Let him eat,
It's been three years, he doesn't want to talk."
A temporary rescue, then it started,
A drumroll of silence awaiting my reply.

It may have been a father's pride and yet,
I sensed he also wanted vindication.
In World War I he served for just two months;
A hardship discharge, mother sick at home.

Now his son a longer run in World War II,
Stage right to London, Air Force, Bombs, Berlin,
The vast scope of the drama thrilled my father;
To me it was vague, out of focus, remote.

My thoughts kept returning to my bunk in England,
In the fetal position for maximum warmth,
Head under pillow to hide from the call-
Soldiers don't fight world wars, only small ones.

In half-round corrugated metal barracks,
Wind blowing in one end, heat out the other,
We fought for spaces near potbellied stoves,
For additional blankets against the cold.

It happened when someone was lost on a mission;
Competition was keen to grab his bedding,
And move his cot away from the fire,
And then the quick move up one place in line.

I reached a high of seven sets of covers,
My bed made chess moves toward the stove;
To me these were major accomplishments,
But the question-what were the medals for?

Perhaps it was because on mission mornings,
I saw Antoine Saint Exupery skies,
And evenings limping back across the channel,
Churchill's alabaster cliffs of Dover.

Perhaps it was because I was so willing
To go foraging for death as ordered,
To calmly drop my bombs and watch them flower,
Five miles below where the red river flowed.

I never saw the enemy or heard him scream,
No blood, no twist of bayonet stopped by bone;
The death I feared was swift and clean,
From German fighter planes, pink puffs of flak.

One night at Blackpool on the Irish Sea,
At rest camp for crews half-through their duty,
As I picked up a cup of tea my hand began to shake;
I quickly put it down.

The eyes of Guernica's horse wouldn't close.
To keep control I formed a wall around
My mind and seldom dwelled on battle scenes,
Knowing I had only to win the barracks game.

As for awards, they issued standard forms;
The service had its reasons I had mine.
But how to tell a father reaching for one
Final chance for glory, that all his son

Can recall of medals for valor are mist-cold
English dawns, moving closer to the fire,
Gathering dead-airman blankets, keeping warm,
Compliments of the Luftwaffe, Third Reich born.

Lee McCarthy (d.)

INTRODUCTION

I must let you know who I am upfront?
No one stir fries who he is so that you can eat it hot.

When introduced, I do not say
Oh, mine was a common law marriage
and then rush to reassure you
...but, it's printed up in Who's Who.
I do not whip out my receipt to prove
I paid as much for my divorce as you did for yours.

Nor do I announce
that, on my son's foot,
the fifth piggy went
Oui, oui, oui, oui, oui, Monsieur
instead of *whee, whee, whee.*
No normal pigs hung out around my child's feet.
I wasn't raising a prodigal son.

Nightmare and chaos have a right to be
what they are.
Everyone says I need to structure those years
which passed in a blur.
How could that help *then?*
In spite of my resistance to Gertrude's inch-thick lipstick
so that Pain can be the first whore to chair a committee
I realize we pay little attention
to strangers who just start talking:

My friend and I were going home after the theatre.
A street person standing on the corner yelled at us.
I dismissed it as some ugly epithet a man stranded in the cold night
might well feel like yelling at a white Lexus streaking past.
Then, for some reason, I knew what he'd said.

I asked, *Are your lights on?*
Already in that nether world where ramps lead to freeways,
Alicia groped. *God, no!* traveled all the way up
from her conservative shoes. We were silent.
It takes time to absorb a humbling experience.

Necessity whispers behind the back of Scraped-Together Luxury
who carries a clutch purse pressed to her chest.
Cinderella had three mothers working for her.
Only one of them bad.
Only one of them dead.
Ophelia had none.
Women wrap themselves in fake fur
rather than give up being animal altogether.

So I am going to tell you who I am.
Wendell Berry said, *Be like a fox,*
who makes more tracks than necessary,
some in the wrong direction.

Each animal makes his own wisdom.
That man throwing himself across the night
at a car rushing past is who I am.

Michael McLaughlin

I HAD A BETTER POEM TO READ

At my mom's memorial service
at Christ Church Episcopal
Portola Valley
I was about to read a poem.
Then I remembered the only time we'd cried together.

The Park Theater, Menlo Park
She'd taken me to *To Die in Madrid*.

To Die in Madrid was about the Spanish Civil War
She'd taken me out of school to see it. She'd never
been a mom like that.

I wanted to share this moment
with the gathering
but had a better poem to read.

Not about how she'd
battled Alzheimer's for ten years
As if every day was her Battle of Brunete
Every breakfast a crawl up Normandy beach.

I had a better poem to read.
No silhouette of a German Heinkel bomber
like the model I'd made in 6th grade.
Nor the Soviet T-26 tank by a Cathedral gate.
No Hemingway trying to horn in or
Garcia Lorca
facing the firing squad.
Bodies in piles, sliding over each other
pushed by a bulldozer's blades.

Nothing about how she'd swept a breakfast bowl
of Valencia oranges onto the floor.
Sobbing.
Then screaming. A few weeks earlier.

I had a better poem to read.

CANTO XI FROM THE BOOK OF DIVORCE

San Luis Obispo, California

It's pay a bill make five phone calls have
a thought die
Pay a bill have five phone thoughts make
a call die
Make a call have five phone bills drive to
store die
Drive to die make a store house have a phone
child sigh
Sigh a phone child eat a bill make a
springtime cry
Cry a paycheck read a bill eat some
crying pay
Make a color color a call smile a smile
eat
Phone a smile fake a paycheck color
son's phone bath bathe
Bash the laundry phone a bed sheet wish a phone girl
ball
Bill a number bind the newsprint smell
some flowers cry
Gas the car up bill the cat food vacuum two
flea thoughts eat
Call the sunset bill a moonrise pace the
kitchen   Breathe.

I DON'T KNOW
Jalal's Voice 9/12

When I hear the whistle for work
I take my coffee
And go to take my gloves
See Mr Tim what I work on today
He say complete the job from yesterday
I start to work
I'm working 20 minutes
a half hour
and he say to me
Don't work. Go home
I tell him why I go home?
He say
You are Arabic
You are Muslim
You don't see what happened in New York
Washington?
You don't see how many people
your people killed?

I tell him I not do nothing. I work here.
I have been here fifteen years
How can I go home?

He say Go pray in your mosque
Go pray with your leader I
don't want you to work here.

For half a minute
or a minute I'm thinking what can I do?

He say, If you don't go, I get the
police for you

I hear that he say
Maybe there is trouble
So I go
I have my check coming the next day
But I don't go get it I'm too scared
I think maybe if I go there
he do something. I
don't know.

D. Jayne McPherson

SAFE PASSAGE

"Anyone pulled from a source longs to go back." Rumi

The whisper inside her chocolate-craving
                        blood rises,
when she asks its delirious drive
            to calculate her blue toes
                    sinking into
rainforest mud
               -more threatened by
someone else's needs than her own
                as if she wears
the elephant's tusk
           and lets them cut
                away at her body
Not surprised, she learns
          that baby elephants
also wake up   screaming
              in the middle of the night
after being orphaned, watching
                their family
        killed by poachers.

She was not pulled but thrown
           to drywall
              before her gut
became her listener,
        held more claim
to memory than sightings.
                Like an elephant,
she may pound the planet
           and never be heard again.
          Who would tend to

the forest winds
          scattering
                    seed-anointed rain water?
Who would call
          this dying
                    a cyclic return
when every carcass
          tolls
                    its safe passage?

Indigo Moor

APOTHEOSIS

There is an extra star in Orion's belt.
I arc my mason jar up through the fading
light and snatch the firefly in mid-pulse.

The heat lightning's a distant sweetness.
Sugar-pink throbs on nimbus clouds
draining from the night's basin. A screech

owl's cry hugs the pine-peaked horizon.
Behind me is an aluminum *whoosh!*
A swing, a miss, a curse.

In firefly baseball, the elusive
lime-green flickerings mock us all.
Blind in the graying, we are forever

doomed to swing where they were.
We swear and corkscrew to the ground.
The tall, uncut grass plays slivered kite

to the evening breeze. Silhouetted, Momma
laughs at every exaggerated lunge, twist, and fall.
Her fingers are Promethean tongs that trap

each cigarette's volcanic ember. But tonight,
there is more flame than heart and hand can hold.
A twelve-firefly lantern pressed to my cheek:

Does my face glow, Momma? Do I shine?
Tomorrow noon, the rusted beak

of the weathervane will swing north.

Momma, summer,
the fireflies.
All gone.

Merilene M. Murphy (d.)

UNDER PEACE RISING

with the thought of gardens
under peace rising
she carried truth water
to the root mouth of his barren bush soul
put friendly wet to the stunted beggar's
thorny torch
to out the scorch of endless empty
he swallowed the idea of wholesome bloom
and rose

IF EVER

if ever no schism
kisses her muddy butt
if ever unity rubs her
varicose niles
and mississippis
or licks her arid wounds
like dandelion cloudburst wishes
all who know
know impatience
but peace comes
longshot out epidemic loss
rides healing out bloodbone hiding
steals children back from mental sterility
so rise up
under peace rise up
you sweet smiling rebel
inside galactic blue green turtle
laugh
you're home
if ever
if ever late peace comes
infinity too comes
healing a three hundred
sixty thousand year teeth cut
and gum numb raw
comes soothe comes science
all was known comes peace late but comes

so rise up
under peace rise up
you sweet smiling rebel
inside galactic blue green turtle
laugh now
you're home

WHY CAN'T WE ALL GET ALONG

because Eric Priestley writes "and all our questions answers"

WHY
this is America
these are the 1990s

WHY CAN'T
we take our paper seriously
the fiction of money jokes us not
but we have the constitution in our hands
crisp bills to cash in on

WHY CAN'T WE
believe in what we trust in
ourselves empowered
death would be sure to get us anyhow
taxman or not
why not us forgive us our
axes against each other
our hanging trees
our mother wombs broken
our drive-bys
our boiler-rooms
forgive us our gas chokes
our starved
our clueless technologies
our illiteracies carved out factories

WHY CAN'T WE ALL
hope
there is hope
and no mystery in self-love lets you wonder
there is hope
and this is the right time
for peace to make history

WHY CAN'T WE ALL GET
together
this is the first time
the fullest time so far
more people in the world than ever before
can read
together

WHY CAN'T WE ALL GET ALONG
the truth finds us seekers
just like water finds its own level
and you just have to be tired
real tired
and ready to admit you're not real sure
of what we would do with all the reinvested
killing time
but willing at long last willing not to kill

Brenda Nasio

in the district

> "someone told me it's all
> happening at the zoo"
> -   paul simon

we could have walked to rock creek park
the hotel john kilpen on ashmead

where the only sounds were the rustle
of blinds (when we opened the window to let

some steam escape) and the gurgle of water
being flushed through old pipes

but we drove.

it was january and snow covered the zoo
where a wooden bear, elephant, lion and

giraffe move as if dancing when the clock
in the tower chimes off key on the hour.

approaching spring and the changing from
storm windows to screens (when the potted

shamrock thrived) rob rented an apartment
on connecticut with a view of the aviary

and the hoofed stock and the conversation
among the animals that occurred nightly

became routine.

Jim Natal

BORDERLINE

Mexico is bleeding people.
I am opening the sky for them.
Some smell of ochre earth.
Some are calloused as paws.
Others just refract light.
A few speak only in breezes.
I can taste the fires
in the kitchens they left behind.
Their cold matches
rattle like dried insects in my mouth.

Martín crossed near Patagonia, Arizona.
I did not open the sky for him.
Instead, I parted the river.
I walk along its banks waiting
for ocotillo to bloom; the manzanita
has such red branches…even now.
Only a *pendejo* or a *bruja* can see
beyond the chain link and flowers
with petals so large
they hide us from *la migra*.

You know what they always say:
"*El viento sobre la tierra tumba muertos.*"
Ah, yes, this land's remorseless wind
does blow away the dead.
Sunshine spills melancholy
as Martín collects rattlesnakes
and puts them in his pockets.
Puma won't sit beside him
when they stop for water—

he will stand only, tell his stories
from a distance, speak of neon cities
in some future north where it will rain
sticky money on them all.

Their haggard map points the way
to intersections with no corners.
But that's the way it is
once you pass *la linea*.
The gash is 2,000 miles long
and all the barbed wire in the world
cannot suture the wound.

Francesca Nemko

A LAMENT FOR THINGS PAST

Here I am
Dying on the vine
Instead of swinging on Vine Street
Number 817 to be exact
Home of the Musicians' Union, Local 47.
Diggin' the sounds in Studio 4
Sittin in with the big band
In the rehearsal hall
Improvising, pencil flying over the page
Words and sound tumbling out.
Here in my place, with the swingers, the singers
The creators of a world of sound.

They drop in, pick up checks
Plan gigs, talk shop
Exchange riffs, new ideas
A constant buzz of energy.
There's where it all happens
And where my Love is waiting patiently
For me to come back.
To embrace me once more
Suck me into her belly
Make me whole again in her depths.

Reinvented, reinvigorated
Returned to my rightful place
The Music – it's all and everything I am.

Harry E. Northup

honeymoon in pismo beach

the ring on my finger
postcards from hearst's ranch,
the monterey aquarium, old
port inn --
the movement in my legs
from highway 101 & 1

a bay memory
salmon butterflied
walks along a clean beach
a sunset seen from the pier
in pismo beach

ducks within reaching distance
the softness of her body

driving the cliffs of big sur
downward on the outside
a test of nerves

pure ocean memory
paws at the whiskers
of the sea otters
brisk bay air
clean motel walls
the best bite of a clam
i ever tasted

i picked up a duck egg
from the parking lot of a 7 eleven
& took it to the bank of a nearby inlet
placed it on the grass

IN MEMORIAM

Today, I walked with a nuance; it has its vocation
& is of the spirit.

Where the muse allows us to go, blesses the spirit.
To not bully or order words around.
To not interrupt words.

Marriage was a waist around her, sheltering.
With her fires & flowers blooming
adoration aside, she shelters our
journey, beckons, subsides, the quarter
moon invites star-shaped sea flowers mighty mist.
What do we have but a road & a sky.
The red sash dashes toward the door & a hand
made of red roses sends childhood pictures.
The nuance is there is no childhood; it's a mint
green flower at the pool's end. For within the opening I
leave the nuance, sit in shadow, face hidden.
Lexington & Kenmore, I look up & all the lights in the sky
are Wanda's eyes.

Marsha de la O

TO THE ONE WHO IS COMING

Already almost April, your birth month,
nine new moons since sockeye salmon
sluiced up the Talkeeta, since the great sow
lumbered into the river, cubs trailing her,

since a man knelt and dipped his paw
into the icy rush, and with one swipe
became your father. Now we set flowers
and twigs in your mother's hair, rub

her feet with scented oil, brew blackberry
tea, pots of it, as much as she wants—
she is suffused with you, child.
You too are full of everything that made you—

the nebula that lofted up your molecules,
the high place hidden in clouds, shifting light,
cottongrass, blood and bone and amber,
the love that set you swimming…

David Ochs

UNCLE SAM

Uncle Sam
Claims to be
a Chris-ti-an

Uncle Sam
took away
the Red Man's land

Uncle Sam
making slaves
of Black Africans

Uncle Sam
sinking low
killing off the buffalo

Uncle Sam
picking fights
says that it's
his Godly right

Uncle Sam
and his constitution
came up with
the 3/5's solution

Uncle Sam
under God, one nation
carried on with segregation

Uncle Sam
dropping A-bombs

on Japan

Uncle Sam
napalming the
Viet-man

Uncle Sam's
people harmed
but cites the right
to bear big arms

Uncle Sam
throwing fits
everyones a terrorist

Uncle Sam
Iraq, Afghanistan
getting ready for Iran

Uncle Sam
in red, white and blue
keep on doing
what you do

Uncle Sam
wants you.

David Oliveira

PASO ROBLES, SAN LUIS OBISPO,
SAN LUIS OBISPO

All our lives we've been told how things work.
Yet we persist in believing we barely age,
until some warm afternoon, we catch, by surprise,
a reflection in a store window,

hardly recognizing who we have become.
We take our turn at this, as if following
one another up a mountain without a clear trail,
our steps heavy from the need we carry

to be somewhere else,
some place we have never been,
and will not know when we arrive.
I think of a child's game played in the car

with my brothers and sisters as Dad drives
to the coast on Highway 41. Beverly
reads aloud a road sign, *Paso Robles 45 miles*,
and a hubcap falls off. At the next sign,

it's my turn. I say *Paso Robles*, then before
anything bad happens, Robert starts repeating
the line below, *San Luis Obispo, San Luis Obispo*,
and the hubcaps stay on. Never again

will any of us say *Paso Robles* without
adding two charms of *San Luis Obispo*;
towns we drive through on the way
to somewhere else, linked

in a small arsenal of protections
with Latin spells from Mass.

We take it as our mission to say
the dangerous words at odd moments,

quickly adding the incantation that saves
someone from bad luck, a preemptive strike
to rid the world of another reason for sadness,
to let us be happy more often than we are.

The way a photograph of a picnic,
kept for years on the dresser, loses
subtle grays in the lawn, and the spread
of the blanket fades into dim folds

of someone's dress until only dark lines
marking the kindness of a smile, or
shadows proving the curve of an eye,
rise from yellowing distance into a face

beautiful beyond the burden of detail;
so small moments of glad luck
stand out in the picture I have become.
In the picture I dream of becoming,

on a beach, the smallest grain of sand visible
between my toes, watching the expanse of ocean
turn to the enormity of sky, there isn't
enough room for all the brown flights of sparrows

I want to remember. I want so much.
Desire hangs from my cheeks in the morning,
pulls with the weight of years—speaks my name
in the music of coffee, the traffic of work—

whispers at me in public places to let my eyes
call to passing faces which don't stop.
Today want follows me as I'm driving
along those same highways of childhood.

Each road sign now points to a place
where I'm missing a friend; and

I want to be like these hills, which are just hills,
skins of straw blades mining August light

for their splendor—no thoughts of travelers
or the roads where every turn is a sadness for someone.
I say I want to go first, but in truth,
I don't want any of us to go at all.

Foolish wants of a person no smarter than myself.
Like magic words, the few tricks I've learned
that charm the universe to my side
to keep pain at bay, only work when they work,

and there remain unavoidable moments
in the elegance of days passing between
light and dark when hurt is all I can do.

JERRY FALWELL CONTEMPLATES ORAL SEX
for William Jefferson Clinton

It must be done in the dark,
so he closes his eyes to imagine it.
Someone passing by at this moment
might mistake his attitude for prayer,
and so it is. The tiny upward turns
at the ends of his mouth
betray a thankfulness that this awful labor
has fallen to him, the faithful spared
from trying to figure God's intention
for the various human orifices.
What God wants has always been harder to know
than what God doesn't.
The proscriptions are so clearly delineated:
no apple; no pork; no donkey; no Bathsheba
The prescriptions need more interpretation:
go forth and multiply; do unto others.
He has revealed why God smote Sodom and Gomorrah
and keeps an eye on San Francisco and Paris.
He has revealed why God is so impatient
to punish sexual infractions
Heaven rushes diseases to Earth
rather than wait for the fires of eternity.
And when he explains to them now, that if
"love thy neighbor as thyself" was meant
to include fellatio, men would have been created
more flexible or the penis longer,
he knows the finely dressed
ladies and gentlemen of his Sunday flock
will bob their heads in agreement.
Count our lucky Starr!
The reverend marches for us,
a general at the head of the army of right
delivering God's chosen country
from one more revolting blow.

A LITTLE TRAVEL STORY

Though it is not cold,
the man puts on his business coat
so that motorists using this remote highway
to return from their weekend at the beach
might recognize his walking
as the temporary inconvenience
of one who had not planned to walk.
But because it is also dark now,
his smile appears in the headlights too late
to change anyone's hurry.
It would be simple, at this point,
to turn your attention
to the hard facts in the lives
of the Mexican farm worker and his pregnant wife,
who are the ones who stop for the stranded driver,
who, in a language he does not understand,
invite him to ride to a telephone
in the back of an old gray truck
with the company of two children.
But this is, finally, not the story of a poor family
who could not think of other than helping,
nor is it a story to show the generosity
of the hapless walker
whose gratitude buys a month's groceries,
nor is it the story of his car
that, for reasons it keeps to itself,
quits fourteen miles from the nearest phone.
This, you will be surprised to learn,
is the old story of the moon
which no one sees rise behind them
in the June night, one day away
from being full above all their fortunes.
When the moon is a ripe apricot,
its glistening sugar easy
to pick off the kiss of a lover,

who thinks the sweetness will last
for just the moment they are tasting?
Even if you stand beside the road
and watch the moon grow small,
aging to white in the span of one night,
you will not understand anymore than you do now
about the roundness that rolls each moment away
from this life you love so much.
It is only this little thing the story wants to tell.
The travelers find their way home.
The moon goes to sleep on the other side of the world.

Enid Osborn

DANCE OF THE DEAD SNAKE

Father gets his pistol from the truck
We tie the horses and follow
Stay back, he warns, feet set apart

and fires two shots. The snake uncoils
and stretches full length, its dry rattle
coming as an afterthought

Father chops the head off with a shovel
buries it with its fangs wet
stamps the small grave with his heel

I ask how the snake still moves
without a head. Mother says
Its nervous system isn't dead yet

I think of The Headless Horseman
riding down with terrible purpose
and wonder if the crawler

means to take vengeance on us
or does it merely repeat the dictates
of the day: Catch a rat, seek shade, follow water

I cannot take my eyes from it
Torture or rapture: the dance is the same
It leaves a mad puzzle in the dust

Brother comes with a long, forked stick
and hoists the beautiful, painted belt
like a penant, proud boy

It dances and writhes in the air
Shall I pity a thing so graceful?
Shall I move in time with its rhythm?

During the night, it drops down
and begins to crawl toward the woodpile
but asks with its glass mind

Shelter from what? and draws
aimless pictures instead

How long will it twist in limbo?
And what heaven shall I pray it to?

Bill Pearlman

FOR LINDA

That time in Coyoacan,
we disembarked on a bus to Frida's museo
and we were at home with her history,
the blessed jacarandas in full bloom

and the blue house was momentarily ours
and we drifted past her pictures and studio,
a wheelchair before her easel
and you were wide-eyed with awe

and the feel for suffering and art,
of days that both thrilled and pained
the constant search for plenty amid loss
and the rising that genuflected before descent

So much we wanted and shared
amid the confusions the past bears,
and the hesitant sense of new beginnings
or the juxtaposition of memory and mystery

Sam Pereira

ELEGY FOR THE ROSES
--for John J. Pereira

The smell of death and candles
Is all I remember today; that
And the fact the priest
Who was from Malta,
Kept telling everyone "Look
At the calmness in his face."
All I saw was the coldness
Of your dark forehead
When I bent to kiss it;
The pale light that came
From underneath your eyelids.
You made me dig weeds
And cut the lawn; water
Those damned roses
In the summer, in the heat.
Your favorites were the red ones;
Wondrous and beautiful,
Like the woman from Texas
Who said yes in 1948,
And gave you me in 1949.
You laughed when my fingers
Bled from the thorns; another
Gift that, now, as old
As you were when you died,
I appreciate. You watched,
As I tasted my own blood,
Blood as red as the Chrysler Imperial
That bloomed every year
On the side of the house. I swore
I would never deal with nature
Again, when I got older, never

Break out in hives from the allergies
That cutting lawn brought on.
I was wrong. I'm grateful.
I miss having to disagree with you
At the table about watering times,
About the Vietnam war,
And about why the comics
You thought funny, I thought
Disastrously dull, about as funny
As the smile the damned priest
Insisted was on your face
In death. Good bye, Father.
I'm going to tell my students now
How good you were; how flawed;
How important. *I* have, so far,
Mastered flawed. I'll show this
To my wife tonight, the one
You never got to know. I'll show
This to my dog. Your crazy son,
The poet, misses you sometimes.
In the middle of the day,
Your crazy son smiles at the music
You left him. Father, the music.
The music smells like roses.

Anne G. Phillips (d.)

THE WRITER

I want to be *that voice* in your ear.

I want to be the voice
of the ancient oak as it crashes
of the possum dead by a road in morning
of the child screaming in a room in evening
of the peasant woman tortured and shot
    in her fifth month
of the warbler returning to a wetland
    that's gone

I want to be the voice
of the elephant shot in the heart
of the bass drowning in air on deck
of the snail foaming its life out on bait.
I want to be that voice in your ear
of the trapped miners, the suicide brother,
the dolphin slowly strangling
    in fishnet.

And the voice
of three dogs romping
of two lovers hugging
of a horned owl passing
of an old woman smiling
of a four-year-old singing
of a thousand frogs shouting
of a baby staring open-eyed
    without blinking

I want to be
    that voice.

A COW RUMINATES ON VEGETARIANISM --
a theological concept

I

       never said

take, eat, this is my body._

Stanley Plumly

LAPSED MEADOWS

Wild has its skills. The apple grew so close
to the ground it seemed the tree was thicket,
crab, and root, and by fall would look like brush
among the burdock and the hawkweed, as if at heart
it had been cut and piled for burning.
Along the edges, at the corners, like failed fence,
the hawthorns, by comparison, seemed planted.
Everywhere else there was broom grass, timothy,
and wood fern, and sometimes a sapling,
sometime a run of hazel; sometimes, depending,
fruit still green or grounded and rotting underfoot.
I remember, in Ohio, fields of wastes of nature,
lost pasture, fallow clearings, buckwheat
and firewood and broken sparrow nests,
especially in the summer, in the fading hilltop sun,
when you could lose yourself by simply lying down.
Who will find you, who will call you home now, at dusk,
with the dry tips of the goldenrod confused
with a little wind, filling in what's left of the light?

LEAVINGS

To walk out of this flesh, leave the body of the bones.
To undress utterly, so that even love and mirrors
and the voice inside your head wouldn't know you.
To write your name in cold blood by a candle
whose flame would fire air, breath, everything,
including paper. To be totally absent from yourself,
from thought of yourself, to forget yourself entirely.
To go out only at night, naked to the soles,
perpetually catching cold, and in fear of footprints
walk on your hands. They'd think *five-toed bird,*
and at the edge of water imagine flight.
But you'd still be walking, if you could,
out of body, out of time, leaving behind, in a wake
of absence, clothes, fingerprints, ashes, words—

CANCER

Mine, I know, started at a distance
five hundred and twenty light-years away
and fell as stardust into my sleeping mouth,
yesterday, at birth, or that time when I was ten
lying on my back looking up at the cluster
called the Beehive or by its other name
in the constellation Cancer,
the Crab, able to move its nebulae projections
backward and forward, side to side,
in the tumor Hippocrates describes as carcinoma,
from *karkinos,* the analogue, in order to show
what being cancer looks like.
Star, therefore, to start,
like walking on the best day of your life
to feel this living and immortal thing inside you.
You were in love, you were a saint,
you were going to walk the sunlight blessing water,
you were almost word for word forever.
The crown, the throne, the thorn—
now to see the smoke shining in the mirror,
the long half dark of dark down the hallway inside it.
Now to see what wasn't seen before:
the old loved landscape fading from the window,
the druid soul within the dying tree,
the depth of blue coloring the cornflower,
the birthday-ribbon river of a road,
and the young man who resembles you
opening a door in the half-built house
you helped your father build,
saying, in your voice, come forth.

Paul Lobo Portugés

MORNING NORTH WIND: KAI-HUI TO HER BELOVED MAO

1

morning north wind grey day
alone in a corner of our bed
cold to the bone yearning
for you my faraway man
has your foot healed?
has your winter coat arrived?
who watches over you while you sleep?
if you die my tears will shroud your corpse
if I die?

2

no letters come through,
I wait, look, nothing.
would I had wings
to hover near you my dear
unable I am sorrow without end

3

I lean on others
dream I welcome the God of Death
curling around my heart
like a poisonous snake
I am misery
have you forgotten me?

4

I pity our children
do you miss them?
they won't grow like others
play in the warm spring
they are ravaged
by the violent storm of revolution

5

oh my beloved
I want to kiss your eyes
you my man belong to me
I want to go to you
come come to me
warm my loneliness
with an open heart
dare I hope?

Changsha, China, 1929

(The Nationalists assassinated Kai-hui after
she refused to renounce her marriage to Mao)

Holly Prado

HUSBAND MURMURING
for Harry Northup

I hear "solar" I hear "arm" I hear my husband who's
sitting on the bed in the bedroom reading his poetry
out loud to himself to all of us I hear poetry not as
what our culture hears as incomprehensible I hear
Harry's soft voice reading himself how lucky we are

to have our own language substance gathered longings
and years of washing our hair using clean towels remembering
how we learned to use knife and fork how later we
read easy words in a sturdy elementary school book mine
had a mysterious Hallowe'enish cover the black orange green
of autumn pumpkins ghosts the Other World which was exactly

what I wanted to step into   I didn't know it would
become my life long task but that it would cost me
we all have to pay for creative mystical imaginative surrender has it
        been worth it

well

my husband is reading his poems to himself to me to our cats
to the world that doesn't hear poetry but does it gets an infusion
of language-magic every time my husband opens his mouth every
time I defy the odds that a little girl from the Midwest could find
her way to an ancient sacred yet daily immediate way of writing

there's a lot to mourn   friends leave the planet one by one by one
there's plenty to bow my head to in ignorance and there's this singular
evening of hearing now only silence from the bedroom the silence
of a man who's given enough for today who turns his page it's his
new book it's full of warm wheat
which grows which keeps growing

PHOTO: POET WITH IMAGINED ANIMAL

she looks startled as if the weight of her hair has reminded her
that we all die even though she's well thought of has published
books received awards been in love and been abandoned she looks
unwilling to give an inch except for the little blank space around each
eye seeking home which isn't the railway station evoked in even the
shortest of her poems I avoid travel I admire those who go it alone
the women who arm themselves with fabulous copious wings of hair
who pack suitcases with steel-toed hiking boots lacy panties novels
written in obscure African languages the erudite gorgeous poets

among us who are after all human too but I think I suspect I sense
that this poet balances on her shoulder a hamster hidden by all
the hair but a definite auburn-furred relatable rodent she talks to
he is childhood he is before-any-of-this-happened he is the way her
eyes still show the little spaces left for foolishness and squeaking

the man not only abandoned her but went crazy so couldn't feel
guilty couldn't ever return this man not only inspired her to write
about trains the way the last meeting took place over and over
near the tracks of something about to careen into the distance
forever he not only shifted her vision away from heaven but he told
her how beautiful she was which made her angry made her hair
grow not only longer but outward yes as wings grow to offer
the hamster a nest

she would not succumb to cliché to beauty she bought those
fierce boots climbed until she was sure she hated him then

had her picture taken for her latest book the photo
a photo of death approaching slowly
in the eye of the camera in the eye where she's most alive

Stuart Presley

You,
of earthy throat,
and trilling

Where
did you learn mystery?

    Can I dive with you into it?

CALIFORNIA THRASHER

There you are

in the shadows

hiding from people getting out
                of cars and
opening gates.

Hello, dark animal.

PORTRAIT

Gregory Ramirez

SUMMONS TO MY FIRST WHITE HAIR

Now that I have spotted you
while gazing in the bathroom mirror,
I wonder if you could convince your peers
Wearing attire black as a judge's gown
To distance me from the boy crying
At the soaked scarf of a molten snowman,
From the teenager dismissing
A squeeze of the bicep from the head coach
As evidence to join the football team,
And from the young man believing
The curly brown lock on the nightstand
Belonged to his soul mate.

Do this, and all of you will witness
A man laughing and dancing
With his children in the living room.
All of you will witness that same man
Use words he stumbled with as a child
To inspire those who appreciate verse.
All of you will witness that same man
Enjoy with his wife a sunset—
Red as her hair when they first met—
Off the shore of a foreign land
Finances deprived him of in his youth.

Ingrid Reti (d.)

THE PISMO DUNES TRAIL

A faint trail curls past
     an ancient boundary stake
     marking   a bygone era,
winds by rust encrusted coke cans
     embedded beneath bush lupine
     preparing to burst into bloom,
struggles through
     thick stemmed grasses hoarding water,
zigzags around sand scoured
     shards of broken glass,
then suddenly disappears
     on a wind caressed hillock.

A yellow butterfly
     casts a minute shadow,
shifting sand
     tangles the dunes,
footprints
     escape into oblivion.

Doren Robbins

UNTITLED CONDITION

With all my millions I rented a Bonneville
but turned back when the brake pedal started smoking.
The ripped-off feeling, the turning around fury.
I was on the verge of losing the grounded feeling,
the heavier part,
the baggy version,
in a gas station half way from Dekora rental agency,
sweating over the brakes,
vengeful about the pre-paid amount.

Did I have to remember that drawing of my might as well have been
      dead father?
What came to kill him already took his clothes and lost them.
His mind was bare.
He still had his slippers on.
My cousin the artist made the drawing. Look at him,
they've given the squid morphine-drip.
He's all salt flats in the flimsy ink bed.
That's his left eye, still closed,
the one that needed a padded metal clip on his glasses to hold the
      eyelid up,
broken from esoteric disease,
the Pacific part of the war.
There's a jeep with a blown off door on the sand in that drawing.

They were up on the computer screen, those,
the mechanical maladies. You're useless looking at them.
Resentful enduring the iced-over look in the brake cylinder.
The mechanism defectanism.
A lifetime of hissing and firing on my own screen.

Whoever sat on a bench outside a garage burned-out behind his
        thoughts like that?
Whoever the spies and riot police were at the time.
Same as this time.
Whoever said disappointment is the lack of resolve
who wasn't petty?
I don't even think it's an emotion.
The entire appeal to incoherence in front of me.
Not a way of not talking about it but not something else.
There's no rescued effect.
You look like one of those uptight mourners. At home you roar.
Exasperated candor making all the sense I get.

Suzanne Roberts

THE SYNTAX OF GRAVITY
Clark Canyon, California

The tug of the rope, reminding you
that the world holds together
by the superstition of safety—
today, you won't fall. Today,
someone holds the rope below,
ready to catch you. Today,
you can defy the physics of gravity,
surrender to the chalky clouds,
the acrylic sky, the canvas of rock.
And, the rest disappears—the arms
and legs bent, then straight, hefting the weight
of their torso. The fingers and toes reaching,
uncurling, grasping, smearing, holding.
The scrape of skin against granite's lips,
the unnoticed blood. You forget even
your breath. From here, you can harness
the wind, the yellow-flowered rabbit brush,
the sage, the lodgepole pines somewhere
below. Gone is the crevice of time,
the slack monotony of what's next.
Imagination replaced by the ridge lines,
the cracks, the spine. The holds, the next
move, the quivering legs, the heart's iambic
singing. Somewhere, the distant fear
of falling. Somewhere, street children sleep
in the sewers to keep from freezing,
a leper begs on the streets. Somewhere,
a father kisses his dead son goodbye,
a soldier shoots to kill. But not here. Gone
is the world and its cold-boned grief.

Sojourner Kincaid Rolle

IN PEACE AND GRATITUDE
Near Painted Cave

In a perfect world,
trees grow straight up -
limbs lifted in perennial worship.

At Pulpit Rock,
beneath a solitary pew,
a tarantula resides
praising the round world.

A lizard, lone like me,
sunning on a solitary boulder.

Purple profusions grow wild here -
spawned by an invisible philanthropist.
grafted onto rocky terrain

Not without sound
avians flitter in solitude
above our proud wandering.

Centuries of ancestral footsteps
foretell our own destiny.

Lo' the sleek manzanita
apothecary to the realm -
keeper of the species.

Caretakers and dandelions in residence
among the trees and rocky nooks,
long the meandering Marie Ignacio Creek.

Lee Rossi

WHAT A DAY! LOOK AT THOSE ISLANDS ANCHORED

> *What hasn't happened isn't everything*
> *Until in middle age it starts to be*
> *- Frederick Seidel*

Varius, what a day! Look at those islands anchored
on the horizon like battleships, the air so clear and hot

the world seems to shrink like a plum going pruney.
And that otherwise attractive woman, her tattooed back

like wallpaper designed by William Morris.
No matter how long it took, I'd be willing to lick

it off. And that old man over there, he's our age.
He should be sipping margaritas with us, buzzed

on tequila and dehydration, baking like funerary
urns in a kiln. Somebody's paying him

minimum wage to wave at drive-by tourists –
a close-out sale at Blockbuster—

EVERYTHING MUST GO. And yet he seems delighted
with his station, adorning the corner of this busy inter-

section with his stringy hair and beard,
the twined and knotted muscles of his arms

tattooed with our generation's secret history.

Semper Fi! Varius, we've become monuments

to our youth, pitted, eroded, corrupt with age.
Listen to the wind, perfumed with the eucalyptus'

rattling blades, Let's pledge allegiance to this moment, like soldiers we never were.

Jerome Rothenberg

AS THE SKY GOES BLACK

fixed in place
or running
half a man
& half
a crazed
machine

he feels himself
becoming
what he ran from
breaking free
of bones
& skin

a solitary
eye
that looks out
at a street
covered
with tiny birds

yammering
chirping
whose screams
call him
to life
& always birds   (Han Shan)

my burden
more than
yours

a life
so poor
& pure

succumbing
to their
sounds
their wounds
will raise himself
by inches

sail aloft
the dream
is over
with our hands
we touch
the earth

beneath us
paw it
watch
in wonder
as the sky
goes black

A PERFECT CIRCLE

the protocol
of light
runs through
the dreamer's
thoughts

I seize it
unmindful
call it
my own
a flash

redundant
burning
kings
of chaos
rising up

from front
to back
the colors
make
a perfect circle

particles
in flight
the forest
with its thousand
birds

no prototype
more real
an actuality
of hidden
life

a fantasy
of animals
like narcoleptic
mice   *(for John Solt)*
& spiders

see
the sidewalk
rise
& strike you
dead

the way
the road
to paradise
recoils
& binds us*   * blinds us

Mary Kay Rummel

FIELD WALKING IN COUNTY DONEGAL

I stumbled upon a fairy fort
a sacred circle of large stones.
The wind a sea surge
in a holly tree,
peacock-tail-shaped crown
turned by wind from a brambly
hedge to an emerald and amber
soon to be flaming bowl
of mysteries and whispers.

Sky a frosted pane, a tumble of crows.
Fox-red bracken feathered
chocolate rabbit holes.

I turned around inside the circle
three times, sun-wise
as my grandmother said.

Nothing happened.
I climbed high, stony Marmore Pass,
stopped at the shrine of St. Columba
its paper prayers flapping in wind,
passed wilted flowers in jars
to the holy well, glint of dropped coins.

Down I gazed on the field
the stones, the fairy tree, the sea
rapt in salty concentration,
and I wondered if the world
could ever be changed
by my shambling, ancient, field-love.

Dixie Salazar

PLENTY

Our table holds plenty--
lace draped old oak laden
with fruits fallen from the
red skies of October--
pomegranates, sour green
apples, persimmons, shine
with life that also holds
plenty of pepper sized
creatures crawled in from the
cold, trying to survive--
specks, some invisible
they dance ecstatically
seeking warmth as we all
do. And yet...a warm hearth,
scarlet rubies bursting
and splattered Pollock like--
staining lips with juice and
Bonnard reds-- puckered for
fruit kisses ripening
on a cobalt plate-- feast
for eyes and mouths, we fill
ourselves and yet...it is
never enough. We need
more invisible wings
blending ochre and wild
red, primary couplings
that feed the gaps in us--
as old as the stories
of hot yellow bile and
cold black, and the old need
to balance the humors

to hold dark in one hand
light in another and
know that plenty alone
can never be enough.

Benjamin Saltman (d.)

THE LAUNDRY

When I was young the sheets
drying in the yard were a fleet
setting sail. From my back steps
I saw the years were moving
pinned in the air, faces drifting through
to speak to me saying open your hands.
I was ready for a wind to blow the yard away.

Daddy and Mamma were making war
in the kitchen over corn meal.
The week before it was the carp
laid out on newspaper
telling a bloody story.
While I held my bony knees
I would not hear them yell
but feel my kneecaps shift
and the wood tremble.

Behind me tables and chairs
gathered for attack.
What entered at my back blew
into the future, hospitals
and twigs rasping at a screen,
my sister's glasses and her punished face
waving with the laundry in the yard.

Waving as the wind tried to tear
my fate from me and leave
the clean smell of emptiness.
My dream was flapping arms down unbuttoned,
the stiff yellow clothespins
would not unclench their teeth

to let me go. But I opened my hands
and released my fifteen year old knees.
Since then I have been flying.

A COOL PLACE

I go out in the morning and rub my eyes.
Who knows what to tell the day?
Some know what to order immediately,
they recognize each other, what is to sell.
I walk under the peach sky on Aura Street
and my thoughts stick from leaf to post
in happy webs. For those who are like me
it's clear now that the bells have turned over,
they have outrung themselves.
For a while there's room in the city.

Who knows the nature of this pleasure must know me.
A corner of being neither fence nor tree nor peach sky.
My young children know it every day
but it's hard being older to keep from holding
all of everything in a blind embrace.
I want to hold a single thing.
It's time to enter a cool place where only a piece
exists, a beer, a chair,
the intimate hands of one person dangerously one person.
To ask, will you sit near me? To say, you're not everyone.

THE PURCHASE

What they needed or wanted yesterday no longer mattered,
it was huge and it stumbled in darkness
from Sears. It was Kenmore,
Its porcelain and chrome immediately subjugated them,
jets and shelves.
They were not materialists, and preferred
not to dwell on something so large.
The house went on quietly nudging the grass
as if nothing had happened.

I've seen people carried away
sucked into heavy doors
without a sound. And yet
it wasn't their fault, they had not actually
wanted what they got.
The uncertain bounds of their desire, together with their incomes
memories and fears of failure,
took away their judgment.
They were vulnerable to large crates.

They struggled to remove hands from pockets
to hold out credit cards
knowing they paid for passage in the wrong direction.
But it was compensation for so many things
that they felt mild hysteria as they signed.
Compensation, as shadows compensate for earth's exposure
to a sun that goes on imposing itself delivering unbearable light.

E.R. Sanchez

ODE TO HOWL (ALLEN GINSBERG)

My generation's skull shines with a special brilliance,
ears pierced for wearing bling,
faces concealed, made youthful by Mac makeup,
not depressed by the bleakness of
a broken staircase made slippery by summer storms.

My generation cheats past textbooks,
the pages don't A D D up quick enough,
ignoring the knowledge that is beyond the History Channel,
thinking life's obstacles are too boring if not uploaded to YouTube,
running from feeling unimportant is comforting
as smartphones film them cramming into a teabag filled with 3DHD
        cameras,
my generation stares at their computer as they are lowered
into a tea kettle filled with scalding water.
The stages of burning skin are purely
for entertainment.

My generation laughs in medicated circles,
sleeping off last night's intoxicant,
frustrated,
because their life will not be exposed by an unauthorized biography,
written by a disgruntled personal assistant,
scrutinized by media while inspiring reality television shows.

My generation stares down at their smartphone,
stepping toward a broken staircase that hangs over Moloch's volcano,
the stairs disappear into a black storm cloud.
Television tells my generation,
it's okay, keep moving,
the stairs lead to success and the rain improves beauty.

Summer storms maintain the slip of the broken staircase,
guaranteeing my generation's fall,
streaming it live onto Facebook while they tweet the approaching
        temperature,
watching themselves falling into the lava
as they stare at their palms wondering why the smartphone is melting,
knowing something is wrong,
yet too distracted to change,
my generation continues
satisfied.

Trinidad Sanchez, Jr. (d.)

LET US STOP THIS MADNESS

Derek Barfield brutally died – brutally died
Clarence Scott brutally died – brutally died
Chester Jackson brutally died – brutally died
a hundred kids brutally died brutally died
brutally died brutally died
S.O.S.A.D (THE WAR ZONE)
Errol Henderson

The bullets from the guns
that massacred the invalids
in San Miguel, El Salvador,
the bullets from the guns
that killed the poet
in Johannesburg, South Afrika,
the bullets from the guns
that kill the actors on TV,
for no other reason
than our own enjoyment,
are the same bullets
from the same guns
that kill the children
in Detroit, Michigan.
The bullets from the guns
that killed Martin Luther King, Jr.,
that killed Mahatma Gandhi
that killed Oscar Romero,
are the same bullets
from the same guns
that kill the children
in Detroit, Michigan
When will it stop?

When will we learn
to listen to the artists
teaching the children
songs of life
songs of liberation?
Let the children
grow into man/womanhood
Let us stop weeping
for the invalids in San Miguel
for the poet in Johannesburg,
for the children in Detroit.
Let us take a stand,
let us stop the bullets
from the guns
that kill our children
Let us stop teaching
the children
that bullets from the guns
are the only way
to deal with life.
Let us destroy the factories
that make the guns
that shoot the bullets
that kill our children.
Let us take a stand
to share life,
to break bread
with each other.
Let us stop this madness...
the bullets...
the guns!

Postscript:
As one of his last acts, the day after Patrick Purdy machine-gunned five children
to death and wounded dozens of others in Stockton, California, Reagan
pardoned a guy convicted in Texas of illegally selling machine guns.
(By Lars-Erik Nelson, Tribune Media Services Inc.)

SPACE POEMS

I.
The space between
Fall and Spring
contains frozen tears,
We call if snow.

II.
The space inside
Spring and Summer
falls ever so gently
into winter.

III.
The space between
Fall and Winter
is full of dead leaves
and ripe apples.

Terry Sanville

THE GOLDEN WEST SALOON

San Luis Creek gurgled behind her,
  but no one heard,
drowned by Merle and Waylon,
  twanging their Wurlitzer wonders
to the insane and the learned.

With back to the wind,
  her corrugated-metal walls
shielded us on lonesome nights,
  from the cold winter fog
of indecision or despair.

A toy store took her place,
  though cowboy-booted ghosts
still wander Higuera Street and
  ask: Is Monty playin tonight?
Or is that jus you hummin?

Steven Sher

JIMI HENDRIX PLAYS JERUSALEM

This morning before dawn the muezzin's
call to prayer puts an end to my sleep—
a well-aimed rock thrown through the screen.
Some distant longing fills my heart.
More than forty summers have passed
since our stoned host in Santa Cruz
startled us awake with Jimi Hendrix's
rendition of The Star Spangled Banner,
the one performed at Yasgur's Farm
once mud and rain depleted the crowd,
a littered field all that remained.
Here lie fields none will forget
so long as hulls of tanks and armored cars
upset these hills. I check the clock:
just after five, the world emerging
with first light: a baby crying
in the apartment behind us,
crows scattering across the pale sky,
cats posturing and hissing for a fight,
and Hendrix, decades removed,
hitting decibels that deaden loss.

Nancy Shiffrin

ON VIEWING PICASSO

His denuding of Velasquez
his elimination of the Dwarf
the woman legs in the air
exposing a hairy cunt
how he turns everything into self-portrait
Bull no longer sacred to the Goddess
a spoiled boy grinning from every line

I thirst for roundness flame humor
these flowers by Georgia O'Keefe
something about vaginas
reduced – rendered postcard size
color intensified – the World
by Kandinsky   the Ape reclining

Jerry Douglas Smith

"GET ON THE BUS" REUNIONS

No cameras, tape recorders, pagers, cell phones. No pens, no metal.
No jewelry, wigs, nothing strapless. No mini skirts, shorts, or spandex.
No hoods, camouflage, forest green or blue denim.
No wallets or purses; bring only a photo ID.

A face tattooed to the back of his shaved head leers menacingly
from the baddest vato in C Block.
Tears flood his real eyes

as he hugs his old mother and father.
They could finally afford the bus trip
up the length of the state.
His father's thick fingers don't want to let go.
His mother showers him with kisses
and a barrage of Spanish.
For the first time he is ashamed to be in stir—
he should be caring for them, but can't.

Trisha, eleven, meets her father for the first time.
She had wondered what he is really like.
Is he different from the old pictures,
the bits and pieces of letters?

He hoped for this day, when his ex-wife allows Trisha to come.
His deepest cut in prison was abandonment by family.
He tears up and smothers her with hugs and kisses.
Trisha beams.

Laughing mothers play cards or Scrabble with sons and grandsons.
One teenage boy finally meets his dad.

My son is my pride and joy!
Other guys here in lock-up don't have that.
After five hours, families re-show their passes
under the watchtower and file out down
the double chain-link and razor wire of the *dog-run.*

Leaning with hands above his head on the inner fence,
a seventy-year-old lifer peers out at them
with the saddest eyes of all.

MURMURS

Two big-eared deer mice and a pack rat watch
from outside the overhang.
Under the rock shelter,
flames flicker.

Feet shuffle sand—
thunder from the drum.
Shadows and firelight
dance the yellow ochres,
black manganese stain
and petroglyphs pecked
into the stone ceiling.

Dark—
dead of night in the cavern,
river music echoes mumblings
of ancient tongues...

Patterns permeate rock:
under the sand
grates a saber-tooth jaw

below—
sand grades into sandstone
lower—
grind the granites

and beneath bedrock—
murmurs a ceaseless

creation

THE FAT MONKEY BAR IN MATLACHÉ
Moon Pies, Boat Gas, Karaoke Six Nights a Week

Red and green lights from the drawbridge
dapple the bay's black, slack tide.
Mosquito fish sip larvae
hatchin' among cypress knees.

Inside, Pine Island regulars shoot pool,
play the shuffleboard machine
and slurp BBQed oyster shooters
smothered in butter n' onions.

We're knockin' back Turbo Dog Ales
at this busthead bar on Burnt Store Road
in between ColonAid Medical
and Pistols n' Panties.

A dollar-store deacon passes out salvation
tracts onto passed-out patrons.
The band's behind ballistic glass 'n chicken wire—
no wonder I suffer from CHS.*

To this portly gal with tattooed bingo-wings drapin'
her biceps, a Granny-nanny's braggin' 'bout
her husband's birthday. She gave him
the usual SUV—Socks, Underwear and Viagra.

Conch ceviche and blackened peacock fillets
makin' my tongue lick my brain;
the barkeep claims manatee
tastes like chicken.

*CHS: Can't Hear Shit

M.J. Smith

ROCK PAINTING ABOVE THE SESPE

In Piedra Blanca, if you look under
the rocks you'll see stars,
the dome of the universe
blackened by eons of fire.
One red ember guided
by a brown wrinkled hand
shoots straight across the sky
to explode in the sun.
One red figure, a man or god,
hangs suspended in the sky
motionless
as if waiting for a signal
to erase the world and begin again.
What rough hands wet this rock
with blood and hematite
and painted this star map?
What eye measured the night sky
and knew its rotation?
And did he then sit back and wait,
knowing his stars would outlast
the world, yet
believing that his world
would begin again.

K.H. Solomon

SPEAKING IN TONGUES

For Jane Elsdon and Jerry Douglas Smith

Prophets yet ply our ways
    speaking in tongues

and pilgrims seek the word
    by the rocks of their faiths,

at arches or pillars of stone
    found in the wild,

at rings of henged megaliths
    tuned to the skies,

at cut and carved marble
    cold made alive,

or within vaulted granite
    piered and with spires.

But at times, in warm places
    away from the crowd,

a few search for pebbles
    cast on the pond

in the ripples of poets
    speaking in tongues.

Dian Sousa

THE FIRST MARVEL RECORDED IN MY PRIVATE CLOSET

The central image is ugly, but so is evolution… at first

The Thing is tiny, hairless, blind.
They feed it poison; it sucks it down but does not die.
It learns to *like* it.

The woman carrying the Thing is a mother.
She's pretty. She sings a lot.
She works in a Beauty shop and all of the women love her.
They bring her good gin and tell her secrets.
She weaves thin strands of those secrets back into their hair
so when people look at them in a certain light, all they see is mystery,
it's worth all the good gin in the world.

The Visiting Doctor has told the mother that the Thing is a tumor.
The mother has two tiny boys. She rubs their fragile backs
and holds their sweet hands. Her husband, the worried Father,
wishes he could invent a time machine and rush his little family
backward to a sunny land of flying fish and cheery elephants.

The terrified Mother feels the Thing growing inside her
like a slowly inflating murderous black balloon
that will eventually raise her just high enough
off the ground so she can wave good-bye
before it bursts and she breaks into big, sad pieces.

The Thing, in its curlicue ears,
hears only a bleak music laced with sobs,
tastes only a dark poison laced with sorrow.
The Thing learns to like this too.

Months later, right before it might be too late,
the real doctor returns from a family vacation
photographing caribou in southwestern Minnesota.
He says, it's not a tumor. It's a baby.

They work fast. Try to make amends.
They feed the mother buckets of vitamins: continents, oceans,
gigantic time-released galaxies of Big Bang vitamins.
On Paul Bunyan sized plates they serve her whole railroad cars
            coated in iron, ten thousand
coral reefs full of calcium, and a Chiquita plantation of potassium.
The woozy, hairless, blind, baby sucks these down too.

Finally, it's plumped-up, big enough to just barely be born:
Girl. Tiny, hairless, nearsighted, not blind, but screaming.
She won't stop screaming, so her father rubs her gums with whisky.
He has to do this three or four times a day until she turns ten.

At school they refuse to teach her read because she smells like booze.
She learns to like this too, it gives her time to learn the bus lines,
the ones that take her to the ocean where she learns to read
the currents and calculate the swells.

Instead of memorizing the Pledge of Allegiance,
she memorizes the blue commands of wind
blowing open the hungry faces of waves.
Her National Anthem becomes the operatic surge
and smack of water on rock.

She puts her hand over her heart and stands up straight
for every wild thing that breaks the surface.
She becomes a patriot of the crashing sea,
and of everything that lurks in the depths and is not crushed.

AIN'T NOBODY GOIN' BACK TO THE FARM NOW

For Lisa Coffman

Again this morning too many animals are dead.
The raccoon is slack mouth, bleeding, belly-up.
The small deer's neck is twisted.
Two blood-encrusted squirrels,
a possum, and a dearly beloved cat—
their little bodies flung and bloated.

We are driving past the carnage
on a road winding harder than a snake
petrified in the act of striking.

My friend wonders why the animals
don't just rise up and kill us.
I don't have an answer.

So we turn around and go home,
lock our doors, hunker around a bottle of Jameson
and wait for the animal revolution.

For the wolf to coordinate with the badger,
the badger with the wallaby,
the wallaby with the shark.
The lethal union of fang and talon,
tooth and muscle.

The guard dogs and the show dogs,
they'll be in on it too,
and the mouse and the hamster
will chew our jugulars efficiently in the night.

Our babies will never be safe again
unless they are sleeping
in the rolling belly of the anaconda.

We're almost out of whisky.
We can only find baking soda and air freshener.
The animals won't like that.

We can't feed them.
We're too sick to cook them.
We can't even apologize in the right language.

We can only sip what we have left
while we wait for the gorilla to rise up with the bear,
with the condor, the bull, and the donkey too.

We'll break our bottle open, lick the insides
and wait for the animal revolution,
not the one from down on Orwell's farm
where the poor animals turn ugly—into us.

But the one, rocked and raised and fed by the earth,
coming because its Mama told it to.
The raw and ragged revolution
of horn and beak, scale and claw,
screeching and growling and scratching
at our thinning walls and frail back door.

Gabriel Spera

SONNET (With Children)

My love is like a deep and placid lake...
Not now, sweetie, Daddy's busy, OK?
OK: my love's a deep and peaceful lake...
Here, Daddy can fix it. All better. Now go play.
Um, my love, yes—a rose that blooms in spring...
You tell her Daddy says she has to share.
My love's.... My love's a lake that blooms—no, that springs...
On the wall?! Her what?! No, wait—I'll be right there.
OK—love, lake, spring, joy, flower bedding...
And why is the house so quiet now, I wonder?
Ah, fuck it! (Whoops! Don't say that!) You know where I'm heading.
Don't touch a thing—I need to get the plunger!
Forgive me, love, but time, as you know, is ticking.
So here: no you, no joy, no life. No kidding.

David St. John

COAST POPPIES

The sea air blues the sheer cliffs
Rising up from the shaggy foam below
To these narrow terraces of blowing orange masks
Tiny paper faces nodding on their stalks
& as we walk the snaking muddy trail above

The Pacific waves shattering
Against the rocks along the fringe of Little Sur

I want to gather those fields of paper bells
Swaying like fragile Japanese lanterns yes
Just gather as we pass a whole basket
Of crenellated orange lips into my arms
& bury you in them until every move you'd make

Would rustle like this summer breeze
& the soft laughter of poppies

BUMBLE BEE

It was such a Fifties kind of thing
The astonishing sport coat at the back
Of the drop-dead expensive Roman men's store
I'd passed by almost every day just off

The Corso & sure enough it was exactly
My size & it's almost impossible to describe
The vibrating sense of pleasure
The soft lines of alternating butter-&-black

Gave to the haze left in the eye of
The gazer in this case meaning me as I stood
Before the mirror
Smoothing the lapels along my swelling chest

& the woman beside me herself just a little
Breathless turned & said, "Oh honey, oh honey...."

THE OPAL TREES

When I awaken into the dream

Of your body upon my body
I am breathing the fragrant air of
The opal trees where shivering rags
Of light pearlesque the limbs of
Your body upon my body
As I awaken to the moonscape

Of this solitary bed
Still feeling the soft satin of stone
& the blossoms of the opal trees
Littering the sheets of earth beneath me
As their shattered rinds
Swirl through the branches of the dream

Of your body upon my body

SAFFRON

Even the thin tube of Spanish saffron
Sitting on the spice rack above the butcher block
Cooking table seems to glow with the worth
Of at least its weight in gold & today
At the beach a dozen Buddhist monks in golden
Robes stepped out of three limousines
To walk their Holy One out along the dunes

To the water's flayed edge where the sand burned
With a light one could only call in its reddish
Mustard radiance the essence of saffron
& what I remember most of the scene as
The Holy One knelt down to touch those waves
Was his sudden laughter & his joy & that
Billowing burnt lemon light opening across the sky

PRISM (WHITE LIGHT)

Ice & the shadows of ice like the white scar

Of wind upon the world like the dust
Of polar flares strafing the St. Petersburg night

As the saint is laid again upon the grill of

Circumstance above the searing pearl ash until
Even the stars slowly drilling the sky rotate

In their boiling sockets & all hell breaks

Apart its howling white teeth its breath

Ruptured into the rapturous spectrum of
Pain by which we know the hues

Of our passage each one of us still assembling

The complicated palette (as in *Make me
A pallet on your floor*) where sleep splinters

& the rage of the new day again coaxes us alive

Leslie St. John

SHE WASHED MY HAIR

After the corn snake lines to Cornerstone,
a Christian music festival in Bushnell, IL;

after the ska show under the big tent;
after skankin' and cheers and beach balls
bouncing over our heads, the CD case

struck my eye, expelling green iris and lens
to the dirt; after the body-pushing, rope-

tripping, car-maze walk to the first aid trailer;
after the cold vinyl, potholed van ride
to the hospital; after the 2:00am operation

on the Fourth of July, the forty-two stitches;
after my newly divorced father and mother

drove across four states—a pillow barrier
between them to bring me home
to Arkansas, the new room my aunts

assembled from what was still in boxes
in the garage: Monet's lily pads on the wall,

music box on the chest of drawers, winter
clothes in the closet, a gold-leafed gift book
on the nightstand: *He will wipe every tear*

from your eye. He will make the blind to see again.

After the month of casseroles and cards; after
my father's only visit, two-dozen stargazer lilies;

after Dr. Medcliff injected
an expandable bubble of gas in my eye
to seal the retina, raise the pressure; after days

of lying on my left side to eat saltine crackers,
drink sprite, stare out the window and watch

summer slip away like an apology,
all the while trying not to cough
or sneeze or hiccup and burst my chance;

after walking to the restroom head bent
like a thin poplar in wind, trying hard

not to disturb the tightrope act in my eye—
that I might see, that I might
keep the eye, face intact;

after Mom raised my lid to drop medicine,
she washed my hair,

untangling rusted screw curls, not with force
as she had after dance recitals
and ice skating competitions, but with care—

a jeweler unknotting a thin gold chain,
rubbing each kink smooth.

Her small hand supported my head
dangling from the foot of the bed,
the other tipping an iced tea pitcher

of water to rinse the shampoo.
So, how to tell her now—

twelve years, two states, one husband,
and three prosthetic eyes later—
she made me feel even this loss as love?

David Starkey

DRUNK DRIVERS OF YESTERYEAR

They were a charming bunch—men mostly,
            in suits and ties, careening toward Scarsdale
in Packards and Hudsons. Sometimes
      they'd plow into a sugar maple, or a little
girl. Nearly always they'd be forgiven:
            for who hadn't tied one on after a long day

      selling insurance or Fuller brushes
            or munitions to our friend and ally,
Ngo Dinh Diem? The women
      were even more endearing, with their slashes
of bright red lipstick, their shrugs
            of silent and befuddled explanation

      as the police helped them from the gasoline-
            scented wreckage, Carol Anne weeping,
weeping in the backseat, the long string
      of pearls snapped and spilled
into the roadway like a scattering
            of someone else's frozen tears.

Lani Steele

HORSE WOMEN

Where are the winged mares?
Heads high, sifting the wind in their nostrils.
Time is passing, memories are being murdered
Under the hooves of centaurs.

I want to be a horse-woman,
Winged, flying through clouds
With children on my back,
Headed for a brave land, where courage
Is measured in daily living, not knightly dying.

Bring me my hooves and wings,
My shining feathers and forged feet,
I am headed for gardens of coral,
Through seas of resistance, roses of intrigue,
To mountains of shelter.

There, my flinty hooves will
Grind lodestone to fable,
Granite to stories and sands
For children to play in.

Away from stallion screams,
Rutting battles and bloodied sons,
The children of women will grow tall,
Strong and gentle, brave enough
For truth, wise enough for beauty.

Hannah Stein

IT IS THE SOUL

that weighs the body down—

like the wine in grapes,
fumes that topple you
to earth—

like the wet in a new clay pot,
the boom of the kiln translating
what's fleshy and yielding—

Without ballast the body

floats, light as the dust it's made of,
motes and electrons sparsely
strewn—

dancers in a hall too big
for the dance, beguiled with northern
lights, with shimmer,
with amnesia—

aching to be found—a hut
to shelter a vagabond—to cluster
ardor in the heart—

to be an *I*—

Lisa M. Steinman

SKATING ON THIN ICE

All I remember about skating as a child
is that we weren't supposed to. Mother

said so. It was years before we read stories
about people falling through the ice & gone

as we were — over & over — in my mother's
fearfulness. At the time, we just wanted . . .

what? The dream of a picture book childhood,
which was never ours, our muscles gliding us

from the log where we encased our feet to head
toward the leafless maples & hickory &

oaks, the overhanging limbs. The ice on the pond
was never smooth enough for gliding: that much

I recall. It was achingly cold. We were
not out of Currier & Ives, but neither did we drown.

Roslyn Strohl

CHRISTMAS IN MEADOW PARK

The sycamore rattles her leaves
-the wind is cold.
The dogs snuffle underneath
look up, noses lifted.
We are all pleased
to be out, alive
in the park:
slack-rope walkers,
bikers, runners, homeless snoozers,
humped into sleeping bags
their heads muffled with hoodies
to block the wind and light.
Round and round we walk
where the horses used to race.
No one is shopping
no one is googling
eyes meet eyes
smiles flash.
Children play.
Two girls carry
a big white plastic horse
four arms wrapped around it.
It gallops stiffly.
They are
whispering their story
over its back:
how they are riding,
riding across the plains,
the grasses rippling, how
they are escaping, or saving,
or returning, or are orphans
with the little brother following,
neighing and nickering
all the way to Bethlehem.

Kevin Patrick Sullivan

WHERE WE LIVE OUR BEST LIVES
from a painting by Patti Sullivan

It glows
the painting
as if from the inside
this abstract in greens – yellows-
whites and browns
the light seems to be coming from
the corner
no -
the center

In the upper left corner
where most of the abstraction
is busy generating the light
that glows from the center
no -
from everywhere

This painting is
is like the artist who
painted it
I know this
because she is my wife
and let me tell you
she glows

And it is in this light
that I live my best life

ROBOT LOVE

I think of Data from Star Trek: The Next Generation
Of R2D2 and C3PO from Star Wars
Of the robot Robbie from Lost in Space
But I'm going all the way back to the Tin Man
From the Wizard of Oz – if I only had a heart
So there he was teaming up with a Scare Crow – a brain
A young woman with a dog – I want to go home –I just want to go
        home
And a cowardly lion – courage yea that's all I need – courage
Notice I said teaming up because for me that is important
We cannot get there from here alone

There is something big as the sky inside you
A blue cloudless sky
An ocean
Inside you are the dreams I look for in my waking

I need your heart – your mind – your courage
If I'm ever to get home where all my life is sweet
Childlike and we are hitting our stride
You and me – all of us together
And maybe some love
Not robot love
But real love–
Yea!
A real human love
One love
One planet
A blue cloudless sky inside you!
Yea!!!
An ocean inside you!

ALLEGRO

For Ann Ream

This is where we enter the dark
This is where we must go it alone
Not really
Just without our beloved Ann

To be in this world under the blue sky
With the wind sometimes howling fierce
Without our core dancer's
Improvisational liturgical moves
Interpreting the word love

Ann - you were always one step ahead of us
The poets – the painters – the sculptors
The musicians – the dancers – all the artists
You were always outstretched towards us
Our Queen leading the charge
Giving all you have in this
Our fight for freedom
This most precious prize
The public expression
Of an Art/Life

Always arabesque Ann
Always the core
This long drawn adagio
This dance of making Art public
Where would we be?
If not for your Allegro

Now your tempo is silent

Oh Ann - I thank you
We all thank and honor you
Art is life
Life should be an art

You were always the core
Here in SLO town – Ann
Always the heart

Patti Sullivan

PLEIN AIR POETRY WITH THE ARTIST
STEVEN R. HILL
for Merilene M. Murphy 1955-2007

The plan was to meet the artist at the train station
I'm to observe him and write about the experience
but there's construction going on – a detour

I end up driving full circle
I wave to my street as I pass it and start again

Having to park a few blocks away
gave me time to take in the morning alone

something about all this has reminded me
of meeting Merilene here for the first time

I can still see her bursting into the station
she's all afro and lanky limbs
decked out in animal prints - a gold velvet coat
and that glad to see us smile

She was here to read at the poetry festival
what's more alive than that
as Jack Kerouac would say "mad with life"

Merilene
you would have loved everything about this day
the early morning fog
the coffee break before we even get started
the anticipation of what will come

Oh, the poem you'd write - how you'd embrace all of it

Just as you would that sun that has finally shown up
offering it's much needed warmth

Wildly - madly.

Phil Taggart

CÉSAR WITH HUERTA TATTOOED ON HIS NECK

This baby faced angry boy/man
runs towards/threatening me

the word *Huerta* is tattooed
across the back of his neck
above a taut white t-shirt
just one of many
ink skin scratches
but it's *Huerta* I remember
with its old school tattoo scrawl

we're in front of Rick's home
César with *Huerta* tattooed on his neck
is scary aggressive taunting him

this is an I-runaway situation
but Rick lives here
this is his front yard

I have to say something

is this man terrorizing Rick
like Gonzo did last year
taking his money
taking his room
knocking him around

César with Huerta tattooed on his neck
charges with hate dripping from his lips

I turn to face him   scared

he stops   turns away

for now

Rosalee Thompson (d.)

LOVE SPOKEN HERE

The Cathedral of Saint Anne
of the Divine Colors
has a Black Jesus
a Mexican Mary
and three California surfers
bearing frankincense, gold and mirth
Weather conditions permitting
the sun at half mast
hitting the hearts of stained glass martyrs
turning it all into dancing prisms
guaranteeing a one way flight
on silver tipped angels wings

Imani Tolliver

these hands

my mother said my hair was like moss
difficult to comb
to keep into the pillow at the crown of my head
so she melted it fine
and pulled, pulled it free from itself
thousands of nooses without the knots

as the years went on
and i became more courageous
i cut the nooses free
gathered and twisted and curled and colored the knots
the forbidden, the embarrassing
the backdoor, the kitchen
into sun, agate, dark rum, fizzy mexican coca-cola
and north african oil with herbs at the bottom of wide,
dolloped vases
warm glass, beginning as teardrops
fallen now, have been the colors of my hair

i took the stories that made me
out of the scream of my arrival
the vinyl and chrome couch of 1977
in front of the six million dollar man
and the bad news bears on tv
the girl, the mushroom, tiny, hiding
hooded small thing that i was
touched i was, in the worst ways
eating tears, eating doughnuts,
eating anything sweet that would fill me
into someone larger than i could imagine
into someone strong
into backbone and healer

into the visitor who,
if you were not looking
would tell you all about yourself and herself too
into this soft body without children
except the one she holds close between my breasts
that i screamed into making
scream from between the lips that suffered
from between the lips that would not speak
the lips tasted by the lips
that would taste hers

scream, scream, scream
wide open
now, these lips curved, plentiful, fleshy and pink
tell and tell and tell
because they were told to shut up long ago
the voice box
the brown and red voice box held in this neck
that came from two brown necks
and two before that
was called a white girl
an oreo
          who you trying to be, anyway?

they told me the color of my voice
before i was able to get my bearings
before i knew the language to fight back
they told me that i was far away from them
far from who i thought i was
          white girl
          white girl
          you tryin' to be a white girl
but all i knew was my mother's tongue
all i knew came from the alice in wonderland records
that taught me how to read

i tried to abandon
national geographics and dictionaries

pippi and the mysteries and the magazines
for a language that was more acceptable
but my mother tongue, i could not shake
it was a tattoo that i modified, but never abandoned

so i read aloud
listening to the nuances i created
the resonance that burnishes the girl voice
tobacco and time
rum and crying
into this voice you hear now
with its gravel lows and birdlike highs
that sings when no one's looking
to jesus and lovers i trust

i am looking below my knees now
and there are scars
but i have decided
to turn the clusters and stripes
into constellations
into galaxies
i will have the scars, the stars
make an order
something larger than me or my shins
into orion, zeus, mars and leo

so take what shame tried to make
into your hands and turn it into something else
change your color
to pink, to blue, to black
to your wish
into something new
something of your own making

perhaps you will be as lucky as i
when a new friend remarks to your mother
    you gave birth to imani?
    no, she gave birth to herself.

Jennifer Tseng

Two Flowers

I loved the wrong flower. Its color
of apples & fire & blood
from a body just opened
by the world's knife.
There was one without color
that waited for me. The one
I should have loved
I could not see.

Small Flock
for Nani

What is it keeps you flying
(a thousand miles in all, a garland
adorning the earth) when one of you falls,
a scarlet flower upon his breast,
when one's hurt wing becomes a rose
of white upon the plains of snow below?
Oh collection of rapidly beating hearts,
you of the circular journey, of the yes
& the no, the relentless diminishment,
the continuous, arduous joining, you
of abandoned nests, ragged, raucous, returning,
you exhausted & beautiful,
unmitigated, migrating crown,
what mystery makes you
hold yourself above
this lowdown earth?

James Tyner

HOME ON LEAVE

He's crapped himself. Again.
    A bottle of whiskey crowns his head,
tall can like a scepter, empty.
    Been home two days, from Iraq,
and friends took him out drinking.
    At least he found home.
He's snoring as I lift him,
    careful to avoid smearing
the wetness on concrete.
    But it's everywhere.
In two more days, he'll be
    back in war. Back in the desert.

I don't undress him
    just let hot water pour
over him, clothes damp,
    stained. He's moaning
now, face contorted in the beginning
    of a migraine headache.
And there should be a point here,
    but there's none, just
a twenty-two year old boy
    drunk until his body loosens,
home from war, leaving home
    for war. And a brother
unable to even undress him,
    just wash shit from face and hands.

Amy Uyematsu

GIANT HONEYSUCKLE
- for Ric, landscape artist

An abstract painting these branches
      that splay and bend
           by an unseen hand

      ~~~

The old ones cluster
      their pale arms
           knowingly entwined

      ~ ~ ~

With dark, smooth bark
      the younger limbs reach
           every new quirk a dare

      ~ ~ ~

High above floats
      a canopy of orange -
           October blossoms

      ~ ~ ~

Elegant disorder
      even my mind
           leaping branch to branch

WHEN YELLOW TURNS TO BROWN

"the high yellow note"
    – Vincent Van Gogh

"In a number of Van Gogh's paintings,
the yellow has dulled to coffee brown…"
    – Los Angeles Times,
"Van Gogh Mystery Solved," February 15, 2011

How the mind opens or slams shut when it's still hungry and raw -
there were two schools of learning where I come from
and mine only had the primary colors of white and non-white.

The meaning of yellow depended on who did the asking –
my girlfriend Lorene Taylor with the long blond curls
or me with straight black hair and skin that changed every summer
from beige with yellow undertones to sun drenched brown.

For Lorene yellow was the innocence of daisies or
      luscious like Marilyn Monroe
but my brand of yellow was permanently tainted with the treachery
of Ming the Merciless, dive bombing kamikazes, and Tokyo Rose,
a history fouled by Hearst headlines and Manzanar latrines.

I didn't know then how Van Gogh used yellow to reveal the night sky
painting straight from his tube of chrome yellow
his sunflowers delivered in thick rapid strokes.

I had to find out on my own that Van Gogh was inspired
by the same Japanese woodblock masters I admire
and in one furious decade he emblazoned his fields, stars,
even self-portraits with "the high yellow note."

My early lessons about yellow left a persistent stain -
I still won't paint its perky hues on my kitchen walls
but like Van Gogh, my eye has trained itself
to feast on yellow everywhere I look.

Patrice Vecchione

WRITING:
THE WHYS AND THE WHY NOTS OF IT

If I didn't write I wouldn't die. Why, that's silliness.
My body is far too strong and determined.
My eyes would still see what they see, this heart too.
Blood wouldn't stop its pulse-work.
Feet wouldn't forget the forest is for wandering through.
Nor would I be less inclined to comment on the beauty
of my husband or the ripple of wind through trees.

If I didn't write, my imagination wouldn't stop its daily
moment by moment insistence, not to make something
out of nothing, but to make a frog out of a prince,
a window out of a wall, a day out of a moment.

Without a pen so frequently in hand, a poem in mind,
a phrase turned round and round in my mouth like a smooth
and slippery stone, my imagination wouldn't harden into the gray,
flat matter of reason. I wouldn't forget to notice and proclaim.
Still I'd be a diviner.

Or would I? If I didn't write, would I give up my song, forget
its necessity, speech that for years I begged for, clumsily stuttered,
then thrust my way into?
If I didn't write, would my imagination
would atrophy, would it get frail and wither?
Would a hard shell form around my ribcage, a gnarled claw
overtake my pencil-holding hand?

My eyes would become veiled and darkly hooded.
Scales would bend my back, and my tongue
thickening into a knot that not even the nimblest sailor
would be able to untie.

Jon Veinberg

PIGEON IN A PALM TREE AT ROEDING PARK

I fly up here each day at dusk after the squadron of hawks has veered
off down the railroad tracks to scavenge the boxcars full of dead
chickens and grain, and just before that black-nerved and soulless owl
makes its rounds under the bobbing stars, before the sky turns dark
as a coma. I come here to watch the thin fabric of earth turn a
different shade of green, to hear the snoring breath of God while he
naps, and to erase the thoughts of death I've built up throughout the
day—the kid slinging darts, the cat that lunges from out of the
bushes, the escaped goose pecking at my eye while I forage the
ground for sesame twigs and thistle seeds. Earlier a Frisbee
whooshed my throat feathers right in the middle of my cooing. It is
as solemn as lent when the low-riders wax their cars under the biscuit
of a full moon. Their tattooed arms muscling out the blemishes of
their pride until the moon reflects their faces in the shine of the
winged fury streaming atop their hood ornaments. The fountain in
the corner track reminds me of rain and the possibility that I might
live forever, how it buries the leaves into the earth later to return as
trees, how the water bubbles break up the sludge, giving light to
tadpoles and perch, and guppies while uncovering the bodies of
sacked pets. The low-riders roll their cuffs up to feel for coins in their
bare feet. They divide their loot up and throw the pennies back into
the raining fountain. I can read their wishes in the bleeding creases of
their eyes.

Gloria L. Velasquez

ODE TO RODNEY KING

"Has anybody here seen my old friend, John?
Can you tell me where he's gone?
He's freed a lot of people but it seems
the good they die young
I just looked around and he's gone."

"Has anybody here seen my old friend, Martin?
Can you tell me where he's gone?
He's freed a lot of people but it seems
the good they die young
I just looked around and he's gone."

Trayvon Martin
He shot and killed you.
He murdered you
for being African-American.
No justice for Black and Brown men
in Dr. King's America
where the New Jim Crow rules.

"Has anybody here seen my old friend, Bobby?
Can you tell me where he's gone?
He's freed a lot of people but it seems
the good they die young
I just looked around and he's gone."

"Has anybody here seen my old friend, Trayvon?
Can you tell me where he's gone?
He's freed a lot of people but it seems
the good they die young
I just looked around and he's gone."

Coraje
Anger today
Shame
Pura vergüenza
Tristeza
And in Solidarity con mi gente
en Florida,
I join the Uprising
Maldiciendo the George Zimmerman Verdict.

"Has anybody here seen my old friend, Martin?
Can you tell me where he's gone?
He's freed a lot of people but it seems
the good they die young
I just looked around and he's gone."

(The first two stanzas are from the famous song, Abraham, Martin and John, recorded by Dion in reference to the assasinations of President Abraham Lincoln, President John F. Kennedy, Senator Robert Kennedy and Dr. Martin Luther King Jr.)

SONG OF ROSA

Rosa Parks
Eres mi madre.
You are my mother
Hoeing sugar beets all day long
In the fields of northern Colorado.

Rosa Parks
Eres mi abuela.
You are my grandmother
Crossing the demon river with her children
To create a better life.

Rosa Parks
Eres la mujer fronteriza.
You are the border woman
Enslaved in sweat shops
To feed your hungry children.

Rosa Parks
Eres Zora Neale Hurston.
You are Zora Neale Hurston
Unafraid and daring to cross
The streets in the white part of town.

Rosa Parks.
Eres Dolores Huerta.
You are Dolores Huerta
Beaten and jailed for daring to take on
Agri-buisness slave masters.

Rosa Parks
Eres los rostros de mis nietos
Your are the faces of my grandchildren
Xicano Black and proud
In the crossroads of two cultures.

Rosa Parks
Today I bid you farewell
Honoring your legacy,
Speaking of your courage and strength
To our Black and Brown Warriors of Aztlán.

Performed for Celebrating Diversity Symposium Feb. 6, 2012 at Cal Poly

HEINMOT TOOYALAKET

Chief Joseph,
How could they have shamed you
and your people in this land of plenty,
forcing you into concentration camps,
contaminating you with diseases,
raping your children's identity?

Chief Joseph,
How could they have ignored your greatness
and the suffering of your people,
writing stories about the early pioneers,
Basque settlers,
The Oregon Trail,
Lewis and Clark
While the history of the Nez Percés,
The Piaute
The Shoshone
And other exterminated nations
is neatly tucked away in museums,
DEAD INDIANS on display,
EXTINCT like pre-historic remains.

Chief Joseph,
Today I shed tears of vergüenza
For you and your people
For my Navajo ancestors,
For all my indigenous brothers and sisters
Who remain **INVISIBLE** in this mythical
Land of the **AMERICAN DREAM**.

Chief Joseph,
How could they have shamed you?

Originally written on Oct. 9, 2004 while touring in Ontario, Oregon and Boise, Idaho, Performed for Indigenous People's Month. Another Type of Groove at Cal Poly State University, November 6, 2013

Ken Waldman

HOW WE SCATTER
in memory of Warren Argo

A life may begin in Fresno,
Seattle, maybe Philadelphia,
swing you to Spokane, Juneau,
perhaps Port Townsend. We attend
schools, graduate, take jobs,
quit them, move again. We get
married. Or don't. We have
children. Or not. We make
friends--friends, the existential
as we hug hello, exchange smiles
or tears, waltz ourselves across
continent, feet barely touching floor.

How we scatter as the years
have their way. What's the sound
of an intent engineer steady
on board? A festival of fiddlers
lost in tunes, clawhammer banjos
making clawhammer noise? A proud
dad phoning his girl? What's the sound
of collective joy? How we scatter,
settling from Olympia to Opelousas,
Oakland to Santa Fe to Fairbanks,
finding community ever more fully
in this world. And then the next.

Don Wallis

THOMAS

Gethsemane was hard.
I was so tired of doubting
myself and you, I slept.
And through the days of
your arrest, the trial and the cross
I started doubting
everything you had said.
I need to touch things
and weigh them like
a fisherman does his catch…
or a man hugs his friend.
I've grabbed men
and turned them around
and shaken them and lifted
their robes and sleeves and looked
to see if they had your scars
and wounds. And they don't.
I'm going blind looking
for your face; and deaf
listening for your voice.
It's like I see the darkness
shining with beings of light
beyond the stars
and you entering the room
like sunshine through an open roof…
and you're like the sunlight
through the morning mist
on the Sea of Galilee
singing after the rain.
Solomon, Master,
would never have chosen this.

How can I believe
our Father is our dad;
that he is present, is eternal,
is life itself – and that he guides us
when I don't know
if you're alive or dead?

Viola Weinberg

IT IS THE BEGINNING AGAIN

It is the first day
at the first light
Shall we begin again
on these blankets of
green grass and apple
trees sudden with buds?

If you work too hard, too late
you will miss the majesty of
unstoppable spring
you will drive through the rain
and won't have the time
to stand here, wet and happy

I found the dirt path again
overgrown with mustard
seething with wild garlic
and green spring onions—
the pokes of lilies come up
the seeds of last year reborn

It is the beginning again
it is a time for sloppy tongues
and the sticky, pink embrace
Come with me now - I shall
ruin your schedule and
make you whole anew

COOL ENORMITY

It brushes your cheek in this chamber
coolly, strangely de-oxygenated with
a taste of the sacred, secret bitters
Where does it come from, cool enormity?

There is no choice but to inhale
It's the only breath you will take this afternoon
The worn, tiled floors should be waxed
They should keep their appointments in this place

Other people like you are in those chairs, waiting
lolling like damaged dolls each with one eye up
I take a picture; they don't care
and never once look up, cool enormity

Now you ask yourself, now you let
it crawl all over you as they hit your vein
They ask, "Would you like water," and
you decline, preferring cool enormity

Cool enormity--is it a drug in a bag?
or a woman in a white coat with a caliper?
You are the drumming love in this cool universe
You are the heart-beating, white hole of existence

You will survive, enormously cool

A RETURN TO MONET'S GARDEN

Among the dinner plate dahlias
with their candy-stripes and
russet flags, below the lilacs
the lavish crown on a Japanese bridge
We pose like Claude and Alice--
weathered and seasoned
in our beautiful Borsolino hats
in our finery and nervous smiles
With grown children to share
and grandchildren already in-arms
with the sun pointed midway
on our ornate and strange sundial
We stand here, proving that even
the forlorn, the beaten poets and their poems
from long storms of reality, even those with
pure pain flowing freely from an artery
Yes! Even these poor, shivering birds
in this one mighty tree can fly again
frightened but brave, we both step into
thin air with intense, deeply-held delight
It is afternoon, time to softly coo and croon
it is the long sun on a cold wall of stones
finally - the puzzle has been solved by the puzzled:
Love, when allowed, builds a palace of itself

Jonathan Weinert

MANIPURA, OUT OF TIPHERETH

This fierce horse stumbles from my stable-plexus—
sixteen hands, star both fetlocks, sorrel coat,
no vices, tends to pace when nervous:
      caveat rider.

Earthcurve's grave and gravity, her cure
for yellow cantering. Fever-fled,
she's paddocked in the middle orchard
      facing east and ocean.

Chew that. She craters January pasture,
green shoots creeping under: succulents
and paralytics. A bridle ruse
      can check her.

Her dam's a famous champion, named
for beauty—She's got her eyelights, heat,
and tremor. Smooth her to the sea-fed sky,
      the vital nova.

You'll find she's tried, goes nicely driving double,
foot-clod, clad and roan, her bloodclash spurred
or coaxed with sugar. Keeps her head. Carries
      whom she will.

Jackson Wheeler

KERN RIVER

Light sifts through the leaves of
cottonwoods lining the river
where we stop to stretch
and wade in the swelter
of mid-afternoon.
Ragged walls of canyon
keep us in shadow.
Light shimmers the river's surface,
a smooth break with undertow
between miles of whitewater,
what the river is running *from*
and *toward,* a habit
formed by centuries

You sit on the edge
of the bank, cigarette
between your fingers—
feet in the shallows touch
sandy bottom, feel the current,
the pull from the heart of the river,
pumping itself into frenzy.

It is telling a story, you say,
about a journey, filled with obstacles,
a journey leading home or
into darkness where memory is lost
then found after a thousand lifetimes,
in water brought to the lips,
full of the taste of stones.

For Lee McCarthy

ON OBSERVING TWO CANADA GEESE LANDING IN A POND, SACRAMENTO, CALIFORNIA, AT THE END OF APRIL

Their landing is reveille,
This morning, just past dawn;
The water they trouble
A mirror of sky.

Is there some confusion
As to which blue they belong
Which draws them down?

It is the business of geese
To recognize maps of home.

Their glide and splash
Into the pond's wet open hand
Is called rest,
In the only language they know.

Paul J. Willis

REVENANT

The morning after we put him down,
   our old retriever, the one that limped
   on aging hips—that morning
      a swift coyote, sleek and shining,

bounded down a trail before me
   underneath the eucalyptus.
   I was running close behind,
      watching as he turned his head

and focused his clear eyes upon me,
   ears aswivel—then trotting on
   as if asking me to follow
      into the line of oaks, and then

swerving into the chaparral,
   still looking back, as if we belonged
   to one another, inviting me
      where I could not go.

Rosemary Wilvert

FROM ONE GOLDILOCKS PLANET

...we glimpse
through billions of light years
massive primordial stars
that lived fast and died early

the alchemic furnaces of their cores
crushing hydrogen and helium
into carbon's six protons
eight for oxygen...

iron refusing more fusion
until in cataclysmic collapse
gobbling nuclei
spewing space with gold
and heavier brilliance

swirling into generations of suns
trailing bits into planets

god only knows how many
of mass and orbit "just right"
for water
to bathe molten crust
into eons of blue-green algae

for fins to feet
creeping through phyla
to us the children of time-

"We are made of starstuff
We are a way for the Cosmos
to know itself"
said Carl Sagan

I wonder
is there a way
for the universe to keep us

from erasing
a storybook planet's life

corals…
      honey bees…
           human beings

IT'S MORNING AGAIN

She watches me
reach for my hat

stands on two legs
to put her face into mine
the better to fix me
with her eyes

bounces on all fours
when I find my sunglasses

yawls when I
put on shoes

for another walk

She gallops
the dirt road
to the pond
a timeless race
into autumn

she at seven
me trailing
at seventy

sycamores
turning yellow
grasses dying for rain
She doesn't care

just cries for the joy
of every stick I throw
into the water

No past or future
No thought

of years running out
seven times faster
than mine

CANNON FODDER...

that's what they were
the Frenchman
gestured over the cliff
shaking his head

Seven decades
disappeared
from a broad beach
forever named
Omaha

Clouds obscured
an innocent sun
that morning

No air support
A shore too steep
for the landing craft

In a heavy sea
officers ordered seasick
gear-laden men
Out
into bullet-ridden swells

Those who made it
to shore
crouched for the bluffs

across a mine-laced beach
from hell
using up German bullets
to clear the way
for later waves

though the machine guns
never stopped

until navy destroyers
blasted the bunkers to bits
twelve hours
and two thousand lives
later

the route
cleared for an
American invasion

Nellie Wong

AL CAPONE AND GENGHIS KAHN

Waiting for the No. 12 bus at 14th and Broadway,
The woman in an orange T-shirt and jogging pants
Of periwinkle blue turns to me. She asks:
Are your earrings heart-shaped?
No, I say, they are not,
They're curved arcs with a flattened silver ball.
Oh, hearts are my favorite shapes.
She continues, telling me, a stranger,
That she needs to get to Piedmont near Grand
For her medication for diabetes
And that she's fallen recently several times,
Hurting her right arm and shoulder,
Having come from the "Lower Bottom,"
Where Oakland begins.
Her eyes are shadowed an iridescent blue,
Her cheeks red, her eyes framed
With bangs falling neatly over her forehead.
"Lower Bottom?" I ask
and she says, yes, that's where Oakland begins
Where she lives on 16th Street in a room
Rented from some old people.
And my grandmother was married
To Al Capone for three years, they met
Near Chicago. You know Al Capone?
I nod, nod.
I have quite a family, I'm going to Chicago
In October and will look them up
Though they don't know I'm coming.
I'm on SSI and I'm saving my money,
My room's $200 a month.
I'm part Russian, See my eyes?
She opens them up with her fingers, her eyes

A blue-green, a slight suggestion of her heritage, adding
That she's a descendant of Genghis Kahn,
According to her grandmother who was a genius.
No one has eyes this color anymore, I'm the last.
And are you a born-again Christian?
I say no and she says she was born again
Twenty years ago and she's now 53.
She shifts her body, rubbing her right thigh, glances
Down at her orange leather sneakers,
Her wrists jangling with gold bracelets,
Four necklaces cascading down her T-shirt,
Of opals and stones caged in a brass-net basket.

MAYBE IT'S BASHO

Maybe it's Basho
walking across a stone bridge
the stream rippling full of koi

Maybe it's Jiu Jin
dressed as a man
urging her sisters to rise
and step forward to unite China

Maybe it's Clara Fraser
in her inimitable style
saying," Come on, Sisters,
let's make a revolution!"

Maybe it's the bumble bee
flitting from flower to flower,
the squirrel scampering up a tree

Maybe it's the crowd
amassing in front of City Hall
protesting the California Supreme Court's decision
that only a man and a woman may marry

Maybe it's the government
upholding our right to torture
in the name of homeland security

Maybe it's Oscar Grant
shot face down on a BART platform in Oakland
on New Year's morning,
 no longer able hold his daughter in his arms

Maybe it's the women
 in Congo being raped

Maybe it's the homeless man
Saying if you can for a dollar for *The Street Sheet*

Maybe it's what poetry is
Yannis Ritsos to his brother, Mahmoud Darwish:
…Yet it might also explain our need to share public beauty…

THE RICE NOODLE ROLL MAKER

I'm headed toward Chinatown in Manhattan
My friend and I ride the subway
To Grand St. Station
Ah, Chinatown. My mouth salivates.
It's cool and gray, but the thought
  of enjoying hot and spicy noodles makes me happy
At the corner of Grand and Central,
  my nose follows the odors of chili oil emitting
  from a cart.
A Chinese woman ladles a creamy white liquid-like soup
    into a bucket, spreads
    it into a drawer, shuts it and ladles again
    a scoop of liquid into a second drawer,
    then another, until all five drawers are filled and bubbling
Her kitchen is a set of drawers in an aluminum case
    the size of a bread box
Several customers surround the cart
    waiting for their lunch

An old man watches us, points to a sign:

      Chicken $1.25
      Pork $1.25
      Fish balls $1.25
      Shrimp $1.50

The woman cooks, takes cash and orders:

      Gai, leong gaw order
      Hah, gum yut?
      Siu dee yau? Hai lah!

The fresh noodle flats emerge from the drawer
She folds the corners toward the center,
        fills it with shrimp, then another with pork,

another with fish balls
and sprinkles chopped green onions on the rolls, places them
in take-out sandwich-size boxes.
Working quickly, she shouts out in Cantonese to workers
  Thronging the street

Leong gaw hah, I say, holding two fingers up
Her eyes light up, a smile spreading across her face.
Ai, ngaw hai Hoisan ngin
Ngaw hai Mei Gawk haw gei nin lah!

I respond: *Ngaw gah Bah Bah, Ma Ma Hoisan ngin* too
And you speak *Hoisan wah.* You are so smart! as she rolls up the
                            noodle rolls,
  and showers them with chili oil and Sriracha Sauce
Oh, no, I'm not. I learned at Chinese school,
  But I speak English because Bah and Ma are gone.
  Bah went to Lincoln School, spoke and wrote in English.
  Ma could read the Chinese newspaper and she wrote in English
    to her grandchildren!
Have you learned any English?
No, no, *ngaw um sick Englishee.*

She continues to fill orders for noodle rolls

I sit on a bench in the park and snap a picture of my shrimp noodle
                         roll, remembering
  this immigrant woman making people happy
  with hot and spicy noodle rolls.

J-son Wooi-Chin

GIVE TO ME MOTHER

Give to me, mother, another song
      like the one you gave twenty five years ago
when love dried up like a seed
      and I wanted to go along.
You breathed the fisherman's song
      into a harmonica and gave it to me
to save me from myself.

Those nights the phone rang
      when no one spoke and you heard
that song from London and Paris, then Hattiesburg, MS,
      were not the only times
I returned the song;

I had returned the love others gave me
      when I could no longer use it
and taken back what I'd given them
      when they didn't want it
with that tune, though some never suspected it.

I later learned from brother
      after I placed
a lone frangipani at your gravesite that you had said
      He'd be all right,
He played a lover's song
      with everything on my mind
except flowers.

Give to me, mother, an ancient song
      older than love,
farther than the reaches of immortal sages
      to save me from my life.

I searched the ancient city of Chang'an
    for nine months,
for Wang Wei, the poet you named me after,
    but he had been gone too long.
Still, I wandered the desolate streets
    of Chang'an and Hungzhou
like a lost tourist with nowhere to go.

At Hupei, the city of stones and grey dust,
    I sat on a rock and listened
to the lament of a stone carver, tapping
    his hammer on a burred chisel
all the way down to his lower fingers. For thirty years
    he chipped away at cement glued to red bricks
even as he told me each kink he snapped he brought back
    the chirps of grasshoppers
that pierced the night walls of the Forbidden City
    where dragons and phoenixes still lived.

Toni Wynn

GOOD NEWS FROM THE RIVER

What about that boy,
seven years old,
rescued in the river?

Did you hear his first words
when evening light
hit his calm little face?

I'm thirsty.
And he waved.
Everybody else —

his daddy, his uncle,
his brother — was all right
for hours, bundled dry.

But the boy's uncle
refused to leave the water
'til something was certain

about his nephew in the cabin
of that flipped boat.
The uncle sat

in a dinghy nearby,
just quiet, the whole four hours
the rescue crew worked.

Don't you feel like they
were spirit in the water
then, those two? And

that you want to do that
for somebody,
save or carry them

in deep love?
Stay on the river,
hold the shining space?

Ricardo Means Ybarra

EARL STREET

I always thought Earl Street was the steepest street
in the world even though we all lived at the edge of
Silver Lake and Echo Park on steep streets with a
view of the immense cut where the Red Line
streetcars ran until they tore the rails up
and built the Glendale Freeway.

Earl Street was over the hill on the lake side
up and over the concrete stairway that only us
kids used to explore hidden caves, eat loquats
and toss them at each other before we reached
the top of the stairs and could see
the lake always pristine and blue but encircled
by a high fence, the lake I always wanted to touch.

We went up the concrete stairway in spite of
the view of the lake to see the monkey on a chain
wrapped around a pine tree and secured through
the links by a padlock, a chain about 40 feet long
that almost reached the house and almost reached
us when the monkey would come on all fours and
lunge, pop the chain, pant and spit at the fear
I can still feel when I blink my eyes before he
returned to the pine tree, ignoring us until we
got the nerve to venture one foot or maybe two
into his ground up dust.

2. EARL STREET

Every time we went up and over the concrete stairway
the man with the padlock key tied around a greasy neck
would come out and tell us about the dog that got too close
about the dog tore up under the pine tree
at the back of a house with a view of a
pristine blue lake.

Now, past 50, when I remember myself as a boy
I always think of the monkey,
see him in the mirror, eyes locked on mine
angular square face and no tail,
not a monkee but an ape, snarling as I brush my teeth,
curled fingers searching for the key around my neck
the ape that tore up a dog under a pine tree
and still waits for me on Earl Street
the steepest street in the world.

Al Young

LEEWAY

> *"Consider me,*
> *Descended also*
> *From the*
> *Mystery."*
> *– Langston Hughes*

Time-weary, still, he feels safest winter nights
in the kitchen by the stove. At the back
of his too-studied brain, cave-dwellers groan.
No music, no texts, no ghosts at his side. Just
silence enough to let him listen to the Mystery
from which he's descending. Few ever know;
fewer care. When the pull of phone calls dies
and paramedic fire truck sirens dial down,
he can boil eggs, toast bread, drizzle oil,
peel fruit and thank and see forever into
this moment that staggers, opening endlessly
here into now. Deeper than anything he can
remember, fiercer than any fictitious futures,
pure Mystery stops him cold with warmth.

OH, NO, NOVEMBER, NOT AGAIN!

Nobody knows November better than
all those on whom November zeroes in
real close, real hard. From Mendocino cold
to stark Kern County homelessness, behold
the ways we come at holidays: We scheme,
we borrow, break down, beg & pray & dream.

Why sport November? Try another shot.
Thanksgiving, Christmas, voting year or not,
-- eliminate the holidays. Postpone.
What makes us want to hibernate & groan
about how dark & cold our mornings get?
Just picture Turlock turkeys gobbling wet,
well-doctored feed, an evil meal, their last.
Feast on the breast & meat Novembers cost.
Dig into cooked root veggies, fallen leaves,
& smell the yawning earth; the way she loves
a coat or shawl or sweater fuzzed with lichen.

Time out. Oh, no, November, not again!
Our Veteran's Day (once called Armistice Day),
the Bay of Pigs, the hit on JFK,
Presidio of Monterey, Seal Beach,
Fort Pendleton, McClellan, Travis. "Reach
for the sky, partner. And don't nobody move!"
The stage-coach robs *us* now. Do you need proof?
Nobody knows November better than
all those on whom November zeroes in.

WHAT DECEMBER REMEMBERS

1/
St. Anthony's Dining Hall | Glide Memorial Church, San Francisco

How good it feels always to feed and feed
not really the poor, but actual people, table
by table, more than just one mouth at a time;
next-generation descendents and ancestors,
one by one, one on one, one to one. What fun
to deify and defy, to feed yourself, to last.

2/
*Body Shop El Águila, San Ysidro, with its big sign in English: "MAY WE
HAVE THE NEXT DENTS?"*

Yes, like in *Stormy Monday Blues*, the eagle flew
on Friday and Saturday he went out to play
– except this year's Christmas fell on a Tuesday.
He needed him a hard-work weekend long enough
to knock out a foundry full of fender-benders.
To make ends meet, to lavish, to water his wayward,
can't-speak-Spanish daughters with digital gifts;
to rescue their brother, to win back their mother,
he needed back-busting blessings to lose those blues.
¿La vida loca? Yes, life was still whatever it was,
his sweet and cruel Christmases the craziest.

3/
The Poet at Three

The poet at three crunching on a candy cane,
sucking on an orange. Sandy Claws knocking
back a cold Co-Cola, all sly, all wise, all smiley
and winky, all *White Christmas* dreamy, messing

with the kid: a snowy red picture that sticks.
All the way from Mississippi's Gulf Coast
the poet will clear Cal's glossy golf courses
(Pebble Beach, Hidden Valley, Pelican Hill,
Old Brockway, Coyote Moon, Incline Village)
to land and hang with joy. To and from worlds
he'll get to know, the poet will take heart and give.

YOU SEE HOW SEASONS TWIST THOSE CAUGHT IN THEM

Here in September already you feed
on lean November light, world at your feet,
the summer of your needy slowing shows.

So where if anywhere does autumn fit?
What do we harvest now that time is short?
How can mute light affect the ways we think?

The light and the dark: fall, a falling, equinox.
In San Francisco light the subtlety of change:
about a two-week shift from one to the other.

Some people will get sick during this time,
people often die at dawn or at dusk: transition –
a good time to reflect, reorganize or focus

on sadness (seasonal affective disorder) looking
backward or forward toward winter and hibernation,
where what you see going on sometimes

you really don't want to look at or feel.
Full fall. How do you work with this? West and
the setting sun. Tune in what's going on

in nature. Eat seasonally. Farmer's market.
Not too much fruit anymore, but peppers, beets,
carrots, root veggies. What's growing, what's ripe?

Fruit ripens to root: the clue to what will grow
back into the body as plant; herbal, tonics,
digestive, muscular-skeletal, liver, immunity.

Light freezes dark, soft tendrils harden, a mattress
of sky turns, leaves smother the dew that piles
upon your planted summer loves. You bless daylight.

Bonnie Young

A VERSE OF GARDENS

The slow November sun touches
the green skin of dangling lemons,
sips dew from the final
flush of roses, coaxes me
to the warm side of the patio.
I turn the other way. Where
did this clear meadow of cement
come from? It stretches out,
hopscotched by plots
of Heavenly Bamboo, Bird
of Paradise, and Needlepoint
Ivy tracing stepping stones
out of my flower beds

to a long-ago garden. Here my
father digs for new potatoes,
calls me to share first taste, dirt
rubbed off on his blue bib overalls.
He cuts me a slice
with his pocket knife, sets it
carefully on my tongue
like the first wafer of Holy
Communion, assigning me
the promise and risk
of the garden.

STOPPING BY FOR HOT LUNCH

He pedals in on nice wheels
locks his sweet bike to the chain
link fence. A regular gives
a wary look. In faded camouflage
clothes and cap, he seems too young,
too healthy to be homeless.

In the food line he stares
directly into my eyes, "Nice bike
you have there," I say, *Oh, yeah,*
nice bike, cool car, big house,
beautiful girl. His eyes leave
mine as he swaggers down the line
accepting chicken enchiladas,
rice, beans, salad, vegetables,
choice of desserts and drinks.

When he returns for seconds,
I offer him a clean plate.
He peeks out from under his cap,
holds open a white plastic
grocery bag. *Can I have 'em*
in this? You see, on my bike...

I cringe at the mish-mash of food,
imagine him eating later,
hidden behind a bush along
the highway. I've never seen him
again, but he's moved in with me.

AT RAMONA SCHOOL IN ALHAMBRA

Old paint flakes on the fresh poured
asphalt, stretching from chainlink
fences to shiny trailers.
Mr. Bernal opens the sagging gate
and in they stream, riding the crest
of first-day exuberance, landing
in ports: Miss Rybicki, Fifth,
Mrs. Chen, Sixth, Mrs. Young,
Special Classes. They answer
or nod as I call out Wen-Li Jen,
Carlos Ricardez, Tin Ly,
Man Ying Tam, Angie Woods,
Anh Ho, Venus Valencia.
We chart their points of origin
on the new world map as I sing out,
Cead mile failte, "a hundred thousand
welcomes," and mark Ireland,
my ancestral home. Soon voices
speak softly, *Huan yin, Fuen yan,*
Vui vung, and another,
Bienvenidos a todos,
a strand of pearls
circling us together.

Gary Young

Near midnight, walking by starlight, the ground still wet, the air brisk and moist after the storm, I was startled by a pocket of warm air. A breath from the mountain, the river, the trees? I turned to look. No, the moon.

Last night I dreamed about a bobcat, and this morning I found one sleeping beneath the persimmon tree. I was almost close enough to touch him, when he woke, fixed me with his eyes and disappeared into a thicket. The air was damp with last night's rain. The matted leaves cushioned my steps, and persimmons blazed in the branches of the tree like a hundred suns. I don't know if the cat appeared because I dreamed of him, or if I dreamed of him because he was so near.

In western Massachusetts, a man wandered into the woods to live alone. He tried hunting, but the only animals that stood their ground, the only animals he could catch were skunks. The man was sprayed, of course, but he caught them, ate them, and dressed in a cloak of rancid pelts. When he was found, the scent was on his breath, his skin, and when I heard his story, I thought, comrade.

R. Yurman

THE SPEED OF DARKNESS

"Is the speed of darkness greater
or less than the speed of light?"
— Laurie Anderson

Darkness enters the valley
faster than we can look
between the time the plates are passed
and the food is served
it has grown dark
with only pinpoints of light
from suns so far
they have burned out
before their rays arrive

No matter how fast light travels
darkness gets here first
With the chandelier lit
and the table cleared
a small glow surrounds us
The dark encircles it

ACKNOWLEDGEMENTS

We wish to gratefully acknowledge and thank all the editors and publishers of the journals, anthologies and books where some of these poems have originally appeared.

Sylvia Alcon: "LIKE WHALES, MAYBE" from *Caught in Flight*, Big Yes Press, 2013.
Roger Aplon: "SHE WEARS A SCAR" from *The Man With His Back To The Room*, Barracuda, 2006.
Sara Backer: "THE FOURTH NEST" first appeared in *The Pedestal Magazine, Issue #81*, 2007.
Beverly Boyd: "COMPASS" first appeared in *Slipstream*.
Ivan BrownOtter: "INDIAN TIME" from *Crossing the Plateau*, Penciled In.
Christopher Buckley:"SKY" first appeared in *Pliades* and from *SKY*, Sheep Meadow Press, 2004. "LOOKING WEST FROM MONTECITO, LATE AFTERNOON" in *Five Points* and from *Rolling the Bones*, University of Tampa Press.
George Burns: "FORGIVENESS" first appeared in the *Alaska Quarterly Review*.
Nicholas Campbell: "ELEGY FOR THE LIVING" from *Child of the World – His First Four Books of Poems*, A Phoenix Press Book and previously appeared in Poetry Salzburg Review.
Anne Candelaria: "AFTER SEEING THE TANGO LESSON" first appeared in *if & when*, Penciled In.
Amy M. Clark: "GOING BACK" first appeared in the *Southern Poetry Review*, Fall 2011.
Gail H. Clark (d.): "PIT STOP" from *Pumpkin Fire*, Small Poetry Press, 2001.
Kevin Clark: "LE SECRET" first appeared in *The Georgia Review*, 2007. "INDULGENCE AT MANASQUAN" in *Paddlefish*, 2013. "FLASHBACK AT CASTELFRANCO" in *Kestrel*.
Jeanette M. Clough: "COLD" from *Flourish*, Huntington Beach: Tebot Bach, 2013.
Lisa Coffman: "NOT CHOOSING OTHERWISE" and "BASS" from *Less Obvious Gods*, Iris Press, 2013.
James Cushing: "LAKE TROUBADOUR"; "IN THE RARE MAP ROOM" and "THE FUTURE OF MIRRORS" from *The Magicians Union*, Cahuenga Press, 2014.
Ray Clark Dickson: "THE LAST WHALE" from *Wingbeats After Dark*, Red Hen Press. "THANK YOU FOR THE LAST TIME" from Infinity Press. "THE LADY IN RED" from *Parlando*, K.C. Press, Menlo Park, CA.
Samuel H. Duarte: "AGRICULTURAL LETTERS" first appeared in *Memoir Journal, InVisible Project Anthology*, 2013.
Denise Duhamel: "EXPIRED"; "LITTLE ICARUSES" and "WORST CASE SCENARIO" from *Blowout*, University of Pittsburgh Press, 2013.
Jane Elsdon: "WINTER'S HARVEST" from *Singing Dreams Into Form*, by Beverly Ensing and Jane Elsdon, 1996; *Prayers To Protest: Poems that Center & Bless Us*, Pudding House Publication, 2004, *Urgent Care for the World*, Pudding House Publications, 2004, *Morning and Other Glories*, Iris Valley Press, 2004; *Pause on the Path*, Gene & Jane Elsdon, 2012."ONE MORE NATURE POEM", *Pause on the Path, 2012*.
Clayton Eshleman: "AT THE BRITISH MUSEUM, 11 APRIL 2007" from *Penetralia*, Black Widow Press, 2014.
Landis Everson (d.): "DEATH IS A HOLE" and "THOUGHTS ON HANSEL & GRETHEL" from *Everything Preserved- Poems 1955-2005, Graywolf Press, 2006*.
Peter Everwine: "RAIN" and "AUBADE IN AUTUMN" from *Listening Long and Late*, University of Pittsburgh Press, 2013. "LULLABY" from *From the Meadow: Selected and New Poems*, University of Pittsburgh Press, 2004.

Paul Fericano: "CURLY HOWARD MISREADS EDGAR ALLAN POE" first appeared in the anthology, *A Bird as Black as the Sun*, Green Poet Press, 2011.

Kate Gale: "MEXICAN LIGHT" from *Echo Light*, Red Mountain Press, 2014.

Dan Gerber: "OFTEN I IMAGINE THE EARTH" from *Sailing through Cassiopeia*, , Copper Canyon Press, 2012 and *Poetry*. "REFUGE" from *Sailing through Cassiopeia*, Copper Canyon Press, 2012.

Sandra M. Gilbert: "EARTHQUAKE WEATHER" "MOVING OUT" and "MARCH 13, 2004, SUNSET VIEW" from *Aftermath*, WW Norton, 2011.

Valentina Gnup: "THE CRIES OF ONE CROW" first appeared in Nuclear Age Peace Foundation website 2012, Barbara Mandigo Kelly Peace Poetry Award.

Sam Hamill: "OF CASCADIA" first appeared in *Cascadia Review*. "TRUE PEACE" from *Border Songs*, Word Palace Press, 2012.

Will Inman (d.): "meanings I must almost leave my body" "the argument" and "old Chinese song" from *A Way Through For the Damned"*, Jelm Mountain Press/West,1983.

Rachel Kann: "DAIYENU" first appeared in *A Poets Haggadah, a Passover Anthology*, Rick Lupert, Aint Got No Press.

Karl Kempton: "OF INK" first appeared as a broadside, *Light & Dust*, Kenosha WI.

Steve Kowit: "I STAND IN THE DOORWAY" first appeared in *SUN*. "NOTICE" and "THE BLUE DRESS" from *The Dumbbell Nebula*, The Roundhouse Press, 2000.

Robert Krut: "OUR JOURNEY WILL BE TREACHEROUS" from *This is the Ocean*, Bona Fide Books, 2013.

Tom Law (d.): "BOTTICELLI'S ANGEL" from, *The Long Good Night*, Taproot Press.

Lance Lee: "GREAT UNHAPPINESS GREAT JOY" & "WESTON WOODS" first appeared in *POEM*.

Eleanor Lerman: "WE HAVE OUR DOGS AND THEIR ANCESTRAL BLESSING" from *Strange Life*, Mayapple Press, 2014.

Paula C. Lowe: "JAMIE HERE I AM/TOE HOLD/DUST" first appeared in *burntdistrict*, 2014.

Suzanne Lummis: "EVERYWHERE I GO THERE I AM" first appeared in *The Antioch Review* and from *In Danger*, Heyday Books/California Poetry Series. "LAST REPORTS FROM THE GONDOLA SUSPENDED BY BALLOONS" first appeared in *The Los Angeles Review*.

Glenna Luschei: "COMINGS AND GOINGS" from Presa Press. "WATERMELONS" first appeared in *Askew, Poetry Nook, White Plum Press*.

Adrianne Marcus (d.) "LA BONNE AVENTURE (PAINTING, 1939)" from *Magritte's Stones*, Lapwing Publications.

Jacqueline Marcus: "THE BLACK APPALOOSA" first appeared in *The Brooklyn Review*.

Edward T. Martin: "THE BARRACKS GAME" from *On The Eucalyptus Coast*, Collected Poems.

Lee McCarthy (d.) "INTRODUCTION" from *Good Girl*, Story Line Press.

Michael McLaughlin. "I HAD A BETTER POEM TO READ"first appeared in *if & when;* "CANTO XI FROM THE BOOK OF DIVORCE" in *CRACK*, San Francisco, 1997; "I DON'T KNOW" in *An Eye For An Eye Makes the Whole World Blind- Poets 9/11*, Regents Press, Oakland.

Indigo Moor: "APOTHEOSIS" from *Tap-Root*, Main Street Rag Press, 2006.

Merilene M. Murphy (d.): "UNDER PEACE RISING" "IF EVER" and "WHY CAN'T WE ALL GET ALONG" from *Under Peace Rising*, Woman in the Moon Publications.

Jim Natal: "BORDERLINE" from *Memory and Rain*, Red Hen Press, 2009.

Harry E. Northup: "honeymoon in pismo beach" from *The Ragged Vertical*, Cahuenga Press, 1990.

David Oliveira : "PASO ROBLES, SAN LUIS OBISPO, SAN LUIS OBISPO"; "JERRY FALWELL CONTEMPLATES ORAL SEX" & "A LITTLE TRAVEL STORY" from *A Little Travel Story,* Harbor Mountain Press.

Enid Osborn: "DANCE OF THE DEAD SNAKE" from the forthcoming *A Snake by Any Name,* Big Yes Press.

Anne G. Phillips (d.): "THE WRITER" & "A COW RUMINATES ON VEGETARIANISM" from *Animals and Other People I Have Known,* TM-Renderings.

Stanley Plumly::"LAPSED MEADOWS"; "LEAVINGS" and "CANCER" from *Orphan Hours,* WW Norton & Co. 2012.

Paul Lobo Portugés: "MORNING NORTH WIND: KAI-HUI TO HER BELOVED MAO"forthcoming from *MAO.*

Holly Prado: "HUSBAND MURMURING" & "PHOTO: POET WITH IMAGINED ANIMAL" from *Oh, Salt/Oh, Desiring Hand,* Cahuenga Press, *2013.*

Gregory Ramirez: "SUMMONS TO MY FIRST WHITE HAIR" first appeared in *Cantos,* Vol. 19, 2013.

Ingrid Reti (d.): "THE PISMO DUNES TRAIL" from *Echoes Of Silence,* 1989.

Suzanne Roberts: "THE SYNTAX OF GRAVITY" from *Three Hours to Burn a Body,* Cherry Grove Collections, 2011.

Mary Kay Rummel: "FIELD WALKING IN COUNTY DONEGAL" from *The Lifetime Trembles,* 2014 Poetry Award Blue Light Press, San Franciso.

Benjamin Saltman (d.): "THE LAUNDRY" "A COOL PLACE" & "THE PURCHASE" from *The Book of Moss,* Garden Street Press, 1992.

E.R. Sanchez: "ODE TO HOWL (ALLEN GINSBERG)" first appeared in *Examiner Magazine,* 2012.

Trinidad Sanchez, Jr. (d.): "LET US STOP THIS MADNESS" & "SPACE POEMS" from *Why Am I So Brown,* MARCH/Abrazo Press.

Terry Sanville: "THE GOLDEN WEST SALOON" from *Poems for Endangered Places,*Central Coast Press, 2008.

Nancy Shiffrin: "ON VIEWING PICASSO" from *The Vast Unknowing,* Infinity Publishing, 2013.

Dian Sousa: "THE FIRST MARVEL RECORDED IN MY PRIVATE CLOSET" & "AIN'T NOBODY GOIN'BACK TO THE FARM NOW" from *The Marvels Recorded In My Private Closet,* Big Yes Press, 2013.

Gabriel Spera : "SONNET (WITH CHILDREN)" from *The Rigid Body,* Ashland Poetry Press, Ashland, OH.

David St. John: "COAST POPPIES"; "BUMBLE BEE"; "THE OPAL TREES"; "SAFFRON" AND "PRISM (WHITE LIGHT)" first appeared in his collection *PRISM* published by Arctos Press, ©2002, 2014 David St. John and Arctos Press. Reprinted by permission of the author.

Leslie St. John: "SHE WASHED MY HAIR" from *Beauty Like a Rope,* Word Palace Press.

Hannah Stein: "IT IS THE SOUL" first appeared in *American Poetry Journal.*

Kevin Patrick Sullivan: A previous version of "ALLEGRO" is from *The Space Between Things,* Deer Tree Press, 2008.

Phil Taggart: "CÉSAR WITH HUERTA TATTOOED ON HIS NECK" from *Rick Sings,* Brandenburg Press.

Rosalee Thompson (d.): "LOVE SPOKEN HERE" from *The Music of Women,* Guyasuta/Publisher, 1992.

Jennifer Tseng: "TWO FLOWERS" &"SMALL FLOCK" from *Red Flower, White Flower,* Marick Press, 2013.

James Tyner: "HOME ON LEAVE" first appeared in *Monkey Puzzle,* #7.

Gloria L. Velasquez: "ODE TO RODNEY KING" first appeared in *The Johnstown Breeze*, Vol. 109 No. 30, 2013.

Jonathan Weinert: "MANIPURA, OUT OF TIPHERETH" from *In the Mode of Disappearance*, Nightboat Books, 2008.

Jackson Wheeler: "KERN RIVER" first appeared in *ASKEW* . "ON OBSERVING TWO CANADA GEESE LANDING IN A POND, SACRAMENTO, CALIFORNIA, AT THE END OF APRIL." in *Rivertalk*..

Toni Wynn: "GOOD NEWS FROM THE RIVER" from *Gathering Ground*, Toi Derricotte and Cornelius Eady editors, University of Michigan, 2006, *Ground*, Shakespeare Press Museum, 2007.

Bonnie Young: "A VERSE OF GARDENS", first appeared in *FLYWAY* and *Inside Pockets*, John Daniel, 2009. "STOPPING BY FOR HOT LUNCH" in the *Monterey Observer*, Monterey, CA.

CONTRIBUTORS NOTES

Sylvia Alcon of Avila Beach is one of three founding editors of Big Yes Press. Her poems are in a number of journals and a collection of her work is titled, *Caught in Flight*, Big Yes Press.

Cynthia Anderson – after living in Ojai and Santa Barbara for 30 years, Cynthia Anderson moved to the high desert near Joshua Tree National Park. Her latest books are *In the Mojave, Shared Visions & Shared Visions II,* both available at blurb.com. She is co-editor of the anthology *A Bird Black as the Sun: California Poets on Crows & Ravens.*

Roger Aplon was a founder & editor of Chicago's CHOICE Magazine with John Logan and Aaron Siskind. He's published one collection of short stories, *Intimacies* and nine collections of poetry, most recently, *It's Only TV.* See and hear his work at: www.rogeraplon.com

Jasmine Marshall Armstrong is a native of the Central Coast. Her poetry has appeared in *Sojourners* magazine, *Solo Café* and *Monkey Puzzle* among others. Her poem "The Custodian's Daughter" was selected by U.S. Poet Laureate Philip Levine as the runner up in the American Academy of Poets Introduction to Journals Award. She holds a MFA from Fresno State and is currently completing a doctorate in Interdisciplinary Humanities at the University of California, Merced.

Sara Backer teaches writing at UMass Lowell and leads a reading group in the men's prison in New Hampshire. She is the author of a novel, *American Fuji,* who received fellowships from the Djerassi Resident Artist Program and Norton Island Artist Residency. Her recent or forthcoming poetry publications include *Turtle Island Quarterly, The Arc Magazine, The Rialto, PANK, Asimov's Science Fiction, the NewerYork, Gargoyle and Crab Creek Review.*

Dorothy Barresi is the author of four books of poetry: *American Fanatics,* University of Pittsburgh Press, 2010; *Rouge Pulp; The Post-Rapture Diner,* winner of an American Book Award; and *All of the Above.* She is the recipient of two Pushcart Prizes, the Emily Clark Balch Prize from *Virginia Quarterly Review,* and a Fellowship from the National Endowment for the Arts. Her essays on contemporary poetry appear regularly in *The Gettysburg Review.* She is Professor of English and Creative Writing at California State University, Northridge, and lives in Los Angeles.

Victoria Billings is a part-time innkeeper, part-time copy editor and full-time poet living in Los Osos with her cat and a herd of horses.

Laurel Ann Bogen is the author of ten books of poetry and short fiction. She is a founding member of the celebrated poetry performance ensemble, Nearly Fatal Women. Since 1990 she has been an instructor in the Writer's Program at UCLA Extension, where she received the Outstanding Instructor of the Year Award in 2008. In 2016, Red Hen Press will publish *All of the Above: New and Selected Poems.*

Nixson Borah is an artist and retired art professor. He is a member of Poets on the Edge, and has been a featured reader at most Central Coast poetry venues. His poems have been published in *The Tribune, New Times* and *if & when..*

Beverly Boyd is co-author of the poetry collection *Where Our Palms Rest,* Coalesce Press 2013. In addition, her poems have appeared in such journals as *Caduceus, English Journal, The*

Healing Muse, Poem and *Slant*, as well as the anthology *Voices from the Porch*, Main Street Rag, 2013.

Lynne Bronstein has four books of poetry, *Astray from Normalcy, Roughage, Thirsty in the Ocean* and *Border Crossings*. She works as a newspaper reporter for the Culver City Observer. She mentors adults and children in writing. Poems and short fiction have been published in numerous magazines and web sites. In 2014, she was nominated for a Pushcart Prize for poetry.

Ivan BrownOtter's poems have been published in small anthologies. His book, *Crossing the Plateau,* from his time teaching on the Navajo Reservation, is available at Amazon. Having already lived once, Ivan now writes to gain understanding and perspective.

Christopher Buckley's 20th book is, *Back Room at the Philosopher's Club,* Stephen F. Austin State University Press, 2014. With Gary Young he has edited, *Bear Flag Republic: Prose Poems and Poetics from California,* 2008, and *ONE FOR THE MONEY: THE SENTENCE AS A POETIC FORM,* from Lynx House Press, 2012. He is the recipient of a Guggenheim Fellowship, two NEA grants and a Fulbright Award in Creative Writing, four Pushcart Prizes, and was awarded the James Dickey prize for 2008 from *Five Points Magazine,* the William Stafford Prize for poetry for 2012 from *Rosebud* and he is the 2013 winner of the Campbell Corner poetry contest.

George Burns was the owner of a small company in the semiconductor industry until he retired in 2008. He has been writing short stories and poetry for more than forty years. His work has appeared in many literary magazines, including *Alaska Quarterly Review, The Comstock Review* and *The Massachusetts Review.* In 2003, his poem, *Partly Heliotropic,* was the winner of the Robinson Jeffers Tor House Foundation Poetry Contest.

Nicholas Campbell studied verse writing at Cal State University with Benjamin Saltman and Ann Stanford, where he earned his degree in English Literature. He shared an Academy of American Poets Prize at Cal State Northridge with Jodi Johnson. He was among those selected by William Stafford as one of the winners in the Montalvo Poetry Competition. He taught creative writing at the CMC, Arts Reach at UCLA and seminars at Cuesta College. His book, *Dandelion Clocks,* from Garden Street Press, was published in 1993. He credits his mother, Ann Yatsko Campbell for his interest in poetry. He is a staff writer for *Torrent Folk Magazine.*

Linda Camplese is a Central Coast poet who finds her inspiration from a world out of balance. Her poems attempt to bring subterranean social, political and personal contradictions to the surface. Linda recently had her poem *"My Ladies of the Prairie"* published *in Walt's Corner in the Long Islander.*

Anne Candelaria, Illinois born farmer's daughter, has lived and taught in California for many years. She is a published poet and was chosen 2002 San Luis Obispo Poet Laureate. Many of her poems show her love of place.

Hernán Castellano-Girón was the 2001 San Luis Obispo Poet Laureate. He is a filmmaker, artist and poet now living in his home country of Chile.

Amy M. Clark's book of poems, *Stray Home* from University of North Texas Press, 2010 won the Vassar Miller Prize in Poetry and was a Must-Read 2011 selection by the Massachusetts Council for the Book. Her poems have appeared in the *Writer's Almanac &*

Verse Daily, in the anthologies *Good Poems, American Places*, Viking 2011 and *Old Flame: 10 Years of 32 Poems Magazine*, WordFarm 2012 and in various journals. She grew up in San Luis Obispo and now lives near Boston.

Gail H. Clark (d.) Poems and reviews have appeared in over 100 publications and several chapbooks. We are grateful that Gail made numerous trips to the festival where she always delighted the audience. A native Tennessean, she lived the last several years in the Monterey area where she was active in all things poetry.

Kevin Clark's *Self-Portrait with Expletives* won the Pleiades Press contest. His book *In the Evening of No Warning*, earned a grant from the Academy of American Poets. Clark's writing appears in such places as *Crazyhorse, Ploughshares* and the *Georgia, Iowa* and *Southern Reviews*. His website is: kevinclarkpoet.com

Jeanette M. Clough is a native of Paterson, New Jersey. Her most recent collection, *Flourish*, was published by Tebot Bach in 2014. Recent poetry appears in *Colorado Review* and *Laurel Review*.

Lisa Coffman grew up in East Tennessee and now lives on California's Central Coast – a pair of landscapes that color and inspire her writing. She is the author of two poetry collections, *Less Obvious Gods* and *Likely*. Her work has appeared in numerous literary magazines and anthologies, and has been awarded fellowships from the National Endowment for the Arts, the Pew Charitable Trusts, the Pennsylvania Council on the Arts, and Bucknell University's Stadler Center for Poetry.

Evelyn Cole, MA, MFA, writes novels and poetry because she has to whenever life delights or breaks her heart and she attends critique groups in both genres. An advocate of sound and sense, her poems are easy to understand. Her website: www.evelyn-cole.com

Marguerite Costigan is a professional artist, naturalist, and life-long poet. She began writing poetry as a child on her father's farm in rural Pennsylvania. In high school, her work was published in a national poetry anthology. A 40-year transplant to California, her poems embrace multiple themes: the human condition, the environment, war and love. Her work has appeared in *Pudding Magazine, Café Solo, Asylum*, the anthology *Poems for Endangered Places* and the international magazine *Le Fenetre*. She has also taught with the CPITS Program, and has been reading her work live before Central Coast audiences since the 1970's. Marguerite is the new Poet Laureate for the County of San Luis Obispo 2015-2016.

James Cushing served as Poet Laureate of San Luis Obispo from 2008-2010, during which time he wrote *The Magicians Union*, Cahuenga Press, 2014, from which these poems are taken. Cushing holds a PhD in English from UC Irvine and has been teaching literature and creative writing at Cal Poly since 1989. He hosts a weekly jazz program on the campus radio station, KCPR-FM. Other books include *The Length of an Afternoon, Undercurrent Blues*, and *Pinocchio's Revolution*, all from Cahuenga Press.

Ray Clark Dickson was born in Portland, Oregon in 1919. He has published 12 books of poetry and hundreds of poems including 22 in the prominent Beloit Poetry Journal. Ray was chosen First Poet Laureate, City and County, San Luis Obispo, CA 1999.

Michaelann Dimitrijevich is a songwriter and poet. Being an equestrian, she regards herself as a rider and a writer. Her work has been featured in *Moving Pictures: Nine Los Angeles Poets, Rattle, Spillway, On the Bus, Solo Café, Solo Novo* and she has written and produced a CD of original lullabies entitled *Night Songs*. A native of Los Angeles, she now resides in Atascadero.

Sharon Doubiago is the author of many books of poetry, stories, essays and a memoir. She's a native of California, has lived most of her life on the shores of the Pacific ocean, to which she credits, deepest, the poet in her. Sharon was awarded The Glenna Luschei Distinguished Poet Award by the San Luis Obispo Poetry Festival, November 2009.

Samuel H. Duarte was born in Nogales Sonora Mexico in 1974 and along with his parents migrated in 1980 to California's rich agricultural valley of San Joaquin. His work has been featured in *Differentia Press, La Bloga* and in *Memoir Journal's InVisible Memoir Anthology*, among others. He currently lives in Santa Maria, California with his wife, Jessica, and two sons, Kael and Kaleb.

Denise Duhamel is the author, most recently, of *Blowout*, University of Pittsburgh Press, 2013 and the guest editor for *The Best American Poetry 2013*. A recipient of a National Endowment for the Arts Fellowship, she is a professor at Florida International University in Miami.

Jane Elsdon is author of ten books and chapbooks, her poetry and fiction have appeared in numerous journals and slicks, garnering a number of national awards. She was San Luis Obispo's Poet Laureate in 2005. She lives in the hills of Atascadero with her husband of 60 years, Gene, they have two daughters, two sons-in-law, six grandchildren and a great grandson.

Clayton Eshleman's poem was published in his collection *Penetralia*, Black Widow Press, 2014. Other recent publications include *Nested Dolls*, BlazeVox, 2013 and with A. James Arnold, a translation of Alme Cesaire's original 1939 *Notebook of a Return to the Native Land*, Wesleyan University Press, 2013. Weslayan will publish *A Sulfur Anthology* based on the 46 issues of *Sulfur* founded and edited by Eshleman from 1981 to 2000, in 2014. He continues to live with his wife Caryl in Ypsilanti, Michigan. His website: www.claytoneshleman.com

Landis Everson (d.) was a member of the Berkeley Renaissance of the late 1940s. Landis stopped writing in the early 1960's and started writing again 43 years later. His new poems appear in *The New Yorker, London Review of Books, Poetry,* and *Chicago Review*. In 2005, the Poetry Foundation honored him with the first Emily Dickinson Award, for a poet over fifty who has never published a book of poems. That long overdue book is, *Everything Preserved: Poems 1955-2005*. Landis lived here in San Luis Obispo for several years before stepping back into the poetry community and sharing his work at the festival. He was a dear man and remarkable poet.

Peter Everwine is the author of *From the Meadows: Selected and New Poems* and most recently, *Listening Long and Late*. He is the recipient of the Lamont Award, two Pushcart Prizes, an American Academy of Arts and Letters Award in Literature, and fellowships from the National Endowment for the Arts and the John Simon Guggenheim Foundation. He lives in Fresno, CA.

Paul Fericano is a poet, satirist and social activist. He's co-founder (1980) of the parody news syndicate, Yossarian Universal News Service, and the author of several books of poetry including, *Commercial Break, Cancer Quiz* and *Loading the Revolver with Real Bullets*. In the forthcoming year his work will not appear in *The New Yorker, The Atlantic Monthly & The Paris Review.* www.yunews.com

Adelle Foley is a retirement administrator, an arts activist, and a writer of haiku. Her column "High Street Neighborhood News," appears monthly in *The MacArthur Metro.* Her poems have appeared in various magazines, in textbooks and in Columbia University Press's internet database, the *Columbia Grangers World of Poetry. Along the Bloodline* is her first book-length collection. Beat poet Michael McClure writes, "Adelle Foley's haikus show us humanity. Their vitality and imagination shine from her compassion, from seeing things as they truly are."

Jack Foley has published 12 books of poetry, 5 books of criticism, and *Visions and Affiliations* , a history of California Poetry from 1940 to 2005. His radio show, Cover to Cover, is heard on Berkeley station KPFA, his column "Foley's Books" appears in the online magazine *Alsop Review.* With poet Clara Hsu, he is co-publisher of *Poetry Hotel Press.* In 2010 he was awarded the Lifetime Achievement Award by the Berkeley Poetry Festival and June 5, 2010 was proclaimed "Jack Foley Day" in Berkeley. The Fall 2012 issue of the online *Tower Journal* is a Festschrift for Foley . *EYES,* Foley's selected poems, has appeared from Poetry Hotel Press, and a chapbook *LIFE,* is forthcoming from Word Palace Press. Christopher Bernard has called him "a many – tongued master." Michael McClure has called him, "our firebrand experimentalist , he holds his torch high so the reader can have more light."

Michael C. Ford would rather be respected for what his print and recorded documents are reporting than for any biographic credentials.

Kate Gale is a poet, librettist and independent publisher and founder of Red Hen Press. She holds a B.A. and M.A. and a Ph.D.in English. She has published multiple collections of poetry and written two librettos to two operas. Among other awards, she has won the Allen Ginsberg Poetry Award, the Claremont Graduate University Fellowship and the Mitchell Lathrop Fellowship. Her most recent book is *Echo Light* from Red Mountain Press, 2014.

Dan Gerber's most recent book, *Sailing through Cassiopeia,* Copper Canyon Press won the 2013 Book of the Year Award in Poetry from The Society of Midland Authors. His *Trying To Catch The Horses,* Michigan State University Press, received *Foreword Magazine's* 1999 Gold Medal Book of the Year Award in poetry, and *A Primer on Parallel Lives,* Copper Canyon Press won the 2008 Michigan Notable Book Award. His work has appeared in *The Nation, The New Yorker, Poetry, The Georgia Review, Narrative,* and in numerous anthologies. He and his wife, Debbie live in the Santa Ynez Valley on California's Central Coast.

Sandra M. Gilbert Professor Emerita at the University of California, Davis, Berkeley resident, Sandra M. Gilbert has published eight collections of poetry, most recently *Aftermath.* Her latest prose volume is *The Culinary Imagination,* 2014. Among her other prose books are the memoir *Wrongful Death,* the cultural study *Death's Door: Modern Dying and the Ways We Grieve,* and two essay collections, *On Burning Ground* and *Rereading Women.*

Valentina Gnup received her MFA in Creative Writing from Antioch University in Los Angeles. After living in Santa Barbara for 22 years, she moved to Greensboro, NC, where she taught writing at Greensboro College. In 2011, she won the Barbara Mandigo Kelly Peace Poetry Award from the Nuclear Age Peace Foundation, in 2009 she won the Joy Harjo Poetry Award from Cutthroat Journal of the Arts. Her work has appeared in literary journals including *Nimrod, Mary Journal, Blue Collar Review, Brooklyn Review* and *Crab Orchard Review*. She now lives in Portland, OR.

Jaki Shelton Green is the author of *Dead on Arrival, Dead on Arrival and new Poems, masks, Conjure Blues, singing a tree into dance, breath of the song*. She was selected as the first NC Piedmont Poet Laureate, 2009. Recipient of the prestigious NC Award in Literature, 2003. In 2014 Jaki will be inducted into the NC Literary Hall of Fame.

Jeanie Greensfelder is the author of *Biting the Apple*, Penciled In, 2012. A psychologist, she seeks to understand herself and others on this shared journey, filled as Joseph Campbell said, with "sorrowful joys and joyful sorrows." Poems published in *Riptide, Askew, If & When, Echoes, Orbis, Porter Gulch Review, Vine Leaves* and others.

Sam Hamill is Founding Editor of Copper Canyon Press, where he edited and printed for 32 years while writing more than forty volumes of poetry, essays, and celebrated translations from ancient Chinese, Japanese, Greek, Latin, and Estonian. In January 2003, declining an invitation to the Bush White House, he founded Poets Against The War, compiling the largest single-theme anthology in all of history – 30,000 poems by 26,000 poets- now archived at Ohio State University. His most recent books include *Almost Paradise: Selected Poems and Translations,* Shambhala Publications, *Measured by Stone*, Curbstone Press and *Border Songs,* Word Palace Press.

Michael Hannon was born in California in 1939. He has been writing and publishing poetry for 53 years. His work has appeared in journals and anthologies both here and abroad. His thirty years collaborations with the artist William T. Wiley has produced books, sculptures and numerous gallery and museum shows. He is the author of more than thirty-five titles, including *A Door in the Water, Poems & Days, Ordinary Messengers, Trusting Oblivian* and most recent, *Imaginary Burden, Selected Poems*, Word Palace Press, 2013. Michael is married to Nancy Dahl and lives in San Luis Obispo. He is the father of three lovely boys, now men: Dylan, Jason and Colin. He has three grandsons: Jadrien, Oliver and Kai.

Ginger Hendrix lives and writes in Morro Bay, CA. Her poems have appeared in *AGNI, The Journal, & Crab Orchard Review*. Her book, *Go Make Something Anyway*, if forthcoming in April 2016. She writes the blog wienerdog tricks at gingerhendrix.com.

Angela Hoxsey is a California native who grew up on the Central Coast. A Cal Poly graduate, she worked in the wine industry in San Francisco and Napa Valley for nearly 20 years. She has edited three books on wine and has published poems in a variety of literary journals. In 2006 she started her own company, House in Order, a residential organizing consultancy. A lifelong art fanatic, she recently joined the board of the Arts Council Napa Valley. She lives with her husband, David Hoxsey, in the beautiful Napa Valley.

Kenneth F. Hunter (d.) Poet-musician, friend to many in our community, Ken was a delight to know. His smile and laugh will be remembered above all else. Ken was always welcomed on stage by appreciative audiences.

Will Inman (d.) Will graduated from Duke University and joined the Communist Party in North Carolina in 1947. His major public appearance was before the House Un-American Activities Committee in Charlotte in 1956. He moved to New York City and worked for the libraries. In 1967 he became Artist in Residence at the American University in Washington, D.C. He moved to Tucson, AZ. In 1973 and worked with the developmentally disabled before retiring in 1980. His work has appeared in hundreds of publications and anthologies.

He has published a number of chapbooks including *A Way Through for the Damned, A Trek of Waking,* and *Landscapes Live in Us.* He has read in N.Y., Washington, San Luis Obispo, San Francisco and elsewhere.

Larry Jaffe poets are the doctors of the soul. For his entire professional career, Larry Jaffe has been using his art to promote human rights. He was the poet-in-residence at the Autry Museum of Western Heritage, a featured poet in Chrysler's Spirit in the Words poetry program, co-founder of Poets for Peace (now Poets for Human Rights) and helped spearhead the United Nations Dialogue among Civilizations through Poetry project which incorporated hundreds of readings in hundreds of cities globally using the aesthetic power of poetry to bring understanding to the world. He was the recent recipient of the Saint Hill Art Festival's Lifetime of Creativity Award, the first time given to a poet.

Will Jones is originally from Philly and has lived in San Luis Obispo since 1979. He started writing poetry in the 60's, guided by his creative writing teacher at Susquehanna University, poet Dennis Trudell. Since retiring after a career in public education, Will has been writing more than ever and reading when he gets the chance. Thanks to his wife, Melinda, and his three sons, Devin, Willie and Brady for their inspiration over the years.

David Kann teaches literature and creative writing at Cal Poly and just finished his MFA at Vermont College of Fine Arts.

Rachel Kann shares her poetry at venues such as TEDs, Disney Concert Hall, Royce hall, The Broad Stage and the San Francisco palace of Fine Arts. Her writing appears in journals such *as Eclipse, Permafrost, Sou'wester* and *Quiddity.* She teaches poetry and fiction workshops through the Writer's Program at UCLA Extension. rachelkann.com

Nicholas Karavatos is a graduate of Humboldt State University in Arcata and New College of California in San Francisco. He currently teaches literature and writing at American University of Sharjeh near Dubai in the United Arab Emirates. Of his book, David Meltzer writes "*No Asylum* is an amazing collection of smart sharp political poetry in tandem with astute and tender love lyrics. All of it voiced with an impressive singularity."

Karl Kempton lives happily with his beloved wife, Ruth, in Oceano, California, consciously removed from literary centers. With Kevin Patrick Sullivan, he conceived & co-founded the San Luis Obispo Poetry Festival and Corners of the Mouth, a monthly poetry reading series. His lexical & visual poems have been widely published and exhibited nationally and internationally since the early 1970's; he has 45 titles and poems and visual poems in 40 anthologies. He edited and published Kaldron, An International Journal of Visual Poetry from 1976 to 1990; its current form is found on the web www.thing.net/~grist/l&d/kaldron.htm. His environmental and cultural efforts include working on occasion for and with the Chumash since 1977; fighting commercial pesticide use in his neighborhood for 18 years leading in 2001 to the conversion of 30 acres to a very successful non-chemical vegetable farm that sells produce to its neighbors and customers in the south county; and since 1990 working for a marine sanctuary to protect our local nearshore chumashsanctuary.com.

Klipschutz (pen name of Kurt Lipschutz) is a poet, songwriter and occasional freelance journalist. His work has appeared in the U.S., Canada, the U.K., Ireland and France. Previous collections include: *Twilight of the Male Ego,* and *The Erection of Scaffolding for the Re-Painting of Heaven by the Lowest Bidder.* He co-wrote Chuck Prohet's 2012 international release *Temple*

Beautiful. His new book, *The Drawn and Quartered Moon* was released by Anvil Press (Vancouver, B.C.)2013. He lives in San Francisco, with his wife Colette Jappy.

Steve Kowit lives with his beloved wife, eight cats and two dogs, in the back country hills near the Mexican border. University of Tampa Press published his most recent full collection, *The First Noble Truth.* He refused to fight in Vietnam, taught poetry writing workshops for many years, and is a devotee of Quan Yin. He's the author of the well-known poetry-writing manual, *In the Palm of Your Hand: The Poet's Prtable Workshop,* published by Tilbury House.

Richard J. Krejsa is a past County Board of Supervisor, a retired Cal Poly professor, a nature lover and a vital part of the peace movement in San Luis Obispo

Robert Krut is the author of *This is the Ocean* (winner of the 2012 Melissa Lanitis Gregory Poetry Award), Bona Fide Books and *The Spider Sermons,* BlazeVox, 2009. His poems have appeared widely in print and online; he is also an associate editor for the press/journal H_NGM_N. He teaches at the University of California, Santa Barbara.

Tom Law (d.) was a native of West Virginia. He earned degrees from the University of Michigan. He was a fellow at Johns Hopkins University, a research scientist and professor at the University of Michigan and Claremont Graduate School. He published hundreds of articles and several books on neural systems. Tom was deeply dedicated to caring for his wife Rennie, as she battled Alzheimer's.

Benjamin Daniel Lawless is a San Luis Obispo-based storyteller, designer, web developer and book publisher. He co-founded the literary journal *if&when* in 2013. Learn more about him at www.benjaminlawless.com

Lance Lee's poetry has been published widely in American and English journals. *Transformations,* his fifth volume of poetry published spring 2013, combines interpretative art with his poetry. *Seasons of Defiance,* 2010, his prior collection, placed as a finalist in the 8th National USA Book Awards. *Homecomings* is due out in 2014. Recent and forthcoming publications include Acumen, POEM, Ambit, Chiron Review, Assent and Blue Unicorn. He publishes in other areas too, as with *The Death and Life f Drama* and *A Poetics for Screenwriters,* plus plays and novels. He lives in Los Angeles but spends several months annually with his family in London.

Eleanor Lerman is a writer who lives in New York. Her first book of poetry, *Armed Love,* Wesleyan University Press, 1973, published when she was twenty-one, was nominated for a National Book Award. She has since published several other award-winning collections of poetry —*Come the Sweet By and By,* University of Massachusetts Press, 1975; *The Mystery of Meteors; Our Post-Soviet History Unfolds* ; *The Sensual World Re-Emerges,* Sarabande Books and *The Blonde On The Train,* Mayapple Press, 2009 a collection of short stories. She was awarded the 2006 Lenore Marshall Poetry Prize from the Academy of American Poets and the *Nation* magazine for the year's most outstanding book of poetry for *Our Post-Soviet History Unfolds* and received a 2007 Poetry Fellowship from the National Endowment for the Arts. In 2011, she received a Guggenheim Fellowship. Her first novel, *Janet Planet,* based on the life of Carlos Castaneda, was published by Mayapple Press in 2011. Her latest collection of poetry, *Strange Life,* was published by Mayapple in 2014.

Paula C. Lowe lives on a cattle ranch. Her poems appear in *burntdistrict, Poet Lore, The Iowa Review, Comstock Review, Tule Review, Askew, Dogwood, Sow's Ear* and more. Her latest book is

Moo, Big Yes Press, 2014. And her poems appear in the anthologies *Bird as Black as the Sun* and *Poems for Endangered Places*. Former editor for *Solo Novo*, Lowe is co-publisher at Big Yes Press. She has authored various non-fiction books and holds a graduate degree from the University of Washington.

Suzanne Lummis won the Blue Lynx Poetry Prize and in the fall of 2014, her collection *Open 24 Hours*, will be published by Washington State's Lynx House Press. In 2011, her organization, The Los Angeles Poetry Festival produced a 25 event citywide series, Night and the City: L.A. Noir in Poetry Fiction and Film. In 2013, national Public Radio's "All Things Considered" aired a segment on Lummis and the noir element in Los Angeles poetry.

Glenna Luschei was named Poet Laureate for San Luis Obispo City & County for the year 2000. She has taught poetry classes at Cal Poly, UCLA Arts Reach at California's Men's Colony, Atascadero State Hospital, University of Nebraska Poetry Conference and Saint Andrews College. Her latest project is a book on Willa Cather.

Amy MacLennan has been published in *Hayden's Ferry Review, River Styx, Linebreak, Cimarron Review, Painted Bride Quarterly, Folio & Rattle*. Her chapbook, *The Fragile Day*, Spire Press, 2011 and her chapbook, *Weathering* was published by Uttered Chaos Press in 2012.

Tamara Madison is the author of the collection *Wild Domestic*, Pearl Editions 2011 and the chapbook *The Belly Remembers*, Pearl Editions 2004.Her work has appeared in numerous small press journals and anthologies. Two of her poems have also been featured on Garrison Keillor's Writers Almanac. Tamara is a California native who grew up on a citrus farm in the Coachella Valley. She has two grown children and teaches French and English in a high school in Los Angeles.

Maía. Adder's Tongue Press in 2012 published *The Spirit Life of Birds*, Maía's poems in response to her partner's death. This year she's finishing an eco-feminist science fiction novel, *See you in My Dreams*. She lives in Isla Vista. What keeps her going are close friends, community gardens, the IV Food Co-Op, trees, birds, clouds, stars, music and the endangered, beautiful one ocean lapping all our shores, as Pete Seeger sang to us not so long ago.

Adrianne Marcus (d.) had published over 400 poems, in magazines such as *Solo, Art/Life, Southern Poetry Review, Potomac Review and Paris Review*. As a freelance journalist her non-fiction articles appeared in such food and travel magazines as *Town & Country, Travel & Leisure*, and *California Living.*, She published three books of poetry, several chapbooks and books of humor. Adrienne was a big-hearted person who cared deeply for her family and large household of dogs, including wolf-hybrids.

Jacqueline Marcus is the author of *Close to the Shore*, Michigan State University Press. She taught philosophy at Cuesta College, San Luis Obispo, CA. She is now a contributing political writer for *Truthout.org*.

Edward T. Martin attributes his poetic seed to his all Irish ancestry. He has published two collections and numerous poems. He went from high school to World War II where he received the Distinguished Flying Cross. He then joined the New York City Mounted Police. Along the way, he received a scholarship to pace University and got a master's degree from City University in New York. He has called the central coast home for many years and has read at many of the festivals and other readings.

Lee McCarthy (d.) "I look behind me only when sitting at counters/after midnight in places like Barstow…" from Lee's poem, *Outside Barstow*. Her awards include a Stegner Fellowship at Stanford University in 1974-75 and co-winner for the Nicholas Roerich Poetry Prize for *Desire's Door* in 1991. Lee's writing has appeared in publications such as *Great River Review, Solo and Third Coast.*. Lee was a remarkable poet and intriguing person and is missed by many people, her best friend, Jackson Wheeler first among them.

Michael McLaughlin, a victim of enthusiasms, has written three chapbooks and two novels. He was Poet Laureate of San Luis Obispo, in 2003. Originally from San Francisco, he lives on the central California coast with his brilliant and beautiful wife.

D. Jayne McPherson's early roots in Appalachia, where she was orphaned, then iv-league education, inform topics of recovery and relationships. Her chapbook is *Afterbeats* and small presses like Rambunctious review, north Coast Review, Spillways, and more current publishers. These poems are from her unpublished book, *Orphan at the Well.*

Indigo Moor is a poet, playwright, and author currently residing in Sacramento, CA. His second book of poetry, *Through the Stonecutter's Window,* won Northwestern University Press' *Cave Canem* prize. His first book, *Tap-Root* was published as part of Main Street Rag's Editor's Select Poetry Series.

Merilene M. Murphy (d.) Literary activist, poet and publisher, friend, Merilene left us way too soon. She was raised in N.Y. where she learned firsthand about segregation and speaking up. After moving to L.A., she became active in the arts community in Leimert Park. She dubbed herself "poet-tech" and created the nonprofit "Telepoetics". "Poetry is my way of getting something going, bridging a gap". She helped young people find their way, she was bold, feisty, full of opinions, never seemed to doubt the validity of her own voice. "let me begin as if I were – poet—maker –creator, let me end as if—we are all poets & then all's not lost between".

Brenda Nasio is a poet and writer and mom (Zack, Max and Sam). She has been Assistant Fiction and Poetry Editor for Mademoiselle Magazine, on the editorial staff of The Paris Review and a California Poet in the Schools.

Jim Natal is the Pushcart Prize nominated author of *52 Views: The Haibun Variations, Memory and Rain,* and two previous poetry collections. His work has appeared in many journals and anthologies. The co-founder of the indie publisher Conflux Press, he directs The Literary Southwest series Yavapai College in Prescott, AZ.

Francesca Nemko is a long-time resident of San Luis Obispo, presenting her unique poetry-and-jazz performances at various venues. She recently included singing in her repertoire of talents, combining it with her poetry. Her latest book, published in 2014, is *Transitions: My First 75 Years.*

Harry E. Northup is an actor and a poet. Harry made a living as an actor for 34 years, acting in 37 films including "Taxi Driver", "Over the Edge" (starring role) and "The Silence of the Lambs." Northup has had 10 books of poetry published, the latest being *Where Bodies Again Recline,* Cahuenga Press.

Marsha de la O's first book of poetry, *Black Hope,* won the New Issues Press Poetry Prize and a Small Press Editor's Choice Award. She is the winner of dA Poetry Award and the Ventura Poetry Festival Contest. She has been published in journals such as *Barrow Street,*

Passages North, Solo, and *Third Coast.* She was raised in the Los Angeles area and now lives in Ventura, California where she is co-editor for the literary journal, *Askew.* She is currently working on a novel.

David Ochs grew up (in NYC) with no self-direction, found drugs in my teen and dropped out of high-school twice and college. Joined the army but after 3 yrs. was worse off than when I started. Went to visit an army friend in CA and stayed in self-appointed exile. Worked crappy jobs and lived in studio apts. Went back to school and became a physical therapist assistant and landed a job in a nursing home where I take seniors with dementia for a walk.

David Oliveira is a native of California's San Joaquin Valley. He attended California State University-Fresno, where he studied poetry with Philip Levine. He was publisher and editor of Mille-Grazie Press in Santa Barbara, inventor of *Poet Cards,* trading cards, and founding editor of *Solo.* In 2000 he was chosen Santa Barbara's Poet Laureate. His poems has appeared in numerous anthologies and journals. His most recent book is *A Little Travel Story,* Harbor Mountain Press. In 2002, he moved to Phnom Penh where he is now professor of English at Pannasastra University of Cambodia.

Enid Osborn is the co-editor with Cynthia Anderson of the anthology *A Bird Black As The Sun/California Poets On Crows & Ravens,* Green Poet Press, 2011. Her work has appeared in regional and national journals and was nominated for a 2009 Pushcart Prize. Her collection of Southwest poems, titled *A Snake by Any Name,* is forthcoming from Big Yes Press.

Bill Pearlman's collections of poetry include *Surfing off the Ark, Flareup of Twosomes, Inzorbital, An Elegy for Prefontaine,* and *Brazilian Incarnation 9Selected Poems 1967-2004.* He worked in community mental health in New Mexico, and taught at UNM, Central NM Community College, and Southwestern College in Santa Fe. His book, *Characters of the Sacred,* reflects interests in Jungian psychology, drama therapy and theater. He founded the Zocalo Theater in Bernalillo. He was recently awarded a Philip Whalen Memorial Grant. He currently lives in San Miguel de Allende, Guanajuato, Mexico, where he has been active in International PEN, and started a writer's series, Writers Aloud.

Sam Pereira's latest collection, *Dusting on Sunday,* was published in 2012 by Tebot Bach. He lives and teaches in the central San Joaquin Valley of California.

Anne G. Phillips (d.) After 24 years of teaching English, Anne pursued her own writing interest, first by writing/editing college textbooks and then devoting her time to what she had loved "since the age of six" – poetry. She joined the SLO Night Writers group and eventually entered the public reading world and found that a "ham actor" lived inside her. Pleased when people laughed at her light poems or cried at her sad ones.

Stanley Plumly is the author of 11 books of poems, including, most recently, *Orphan Hours ,* published by W.W. Norton in 2012. Plumly is a Distinguished University Professor at the University of Maryland, College Park.

Paul Lobo Portugés teaches creative writing at UCSB. Books include *The Visionary Poetics of Allen Ginsberg, Saving Grace, Hands Across the Earth, The Flower Vendor, Paper Song, AxtecBirth, The Body Elcctric Journal, The Silent Spring of Rachel Carson, On Tibetan Buddhism, Mantras, Drugs, Breaking Bread and Mao (* forthcoming).

Holly Prado's eleventh book was published in fall 2013, *Oh, Salt/Oh. Desiring Hand ,* Cahuenga Press. Her work has appeared in many literary publications. Her private writing workshops have gone on for forty years, and she has taught for twenty years in the Master of Professional Writing Program at USC.

Stuart Presley grew up in the hills of Parkhill-Pozo. He spent formative years living in a cabin without electricity. Later he went to a one room school and helped homestead the family home. At age 10, he came upon the surrealist book, *Residence on Earth* by Pablo Neruda, and fell in love with poetry and has been writing ever since. His latest publication is *Harvest from the Emerald Orchard* and is currently working on another book with the Emerald Street Poets.

Gregory Ramirez was born, raised and currently resides in Fresno, California with his wife Stephanie and their children Gabriella and Nicholas. His poetry has appeared in *The Broad River review, Cantos, Hawai'i, Pacific Review* and *if&when*, among other publications. He teaches full-time at the Madera Community College Center.

Ingrid Reti (d.) Ingrid taught creative writing and literature at Cal Poly Extended Education, San Luis Obispo. A freelance poet, book reviewer, and editor. Her work has appeared in several anthologies, magazines and two books of poems. In her memory, her family has established a ten year endowment to the San Luis Obispo community if the form of yearly awards in poetry and other writing categories facilitated by the ARTS OBISPO.

Doren Robbins' collections of poetry include *Driving Face Down* (Blue Lynx Poetry Award 2001),*My piece of the Puzzle* (awarded the 2008 PEN Oakland Josephine Miles Poetry Award), and the *Amnesty Muse* (2011 Lost Horse Press). He currently edits, *5_Trope* and teaches at Foothill College.

Suzanne Roberts is the author of the memoir *Almost Somewhere* (Winner of the 2013 National Outdoor Book Award) as well as four collections of poetry, most recently *Plotting Temporality* (Pecan Grove Press 2012). She writes and teaches in South Lake Tahoe, CA. More information may be found on her website: www.suzanneroberts.net

Sojourner Kincaid Rolle is a poet, playwright, an environmental educator and a peace activist. Books include *Common Ancestry,* Millie Grazie Press 1999 and *Black Street,* Center for Black Studies Research 2009. Poems have appeared in *California Quarterly, Coffee Press, Squaw Review* and the anthologies *The Geography of Home, Rivertalk, Poetry Zone I,II & III, The Poetry of Peace,*, and *A Crow Black as the Sun.,* She hosts a monthly poetry event, The Poetry Zone and a yearly tribute to Langston Hughes.

Lee Rossi. Although not as old as the eucalyptus which dot the California landscape, he is among the oldest living transplants to the state. During the 80's & 90's Lee edited the L.A. based magazine *Tsunami,* and more recently he served as a reviewer for ~88~, also based in L.A. His poems have appeared widely and frequently anthologized, for instance in *Grand Passion: The Poets of Los Angeles, Beyond & Blue Arc West: An Anthology of California Poets.* Currently he makes his home in the San Francisco Bay area.

Jerome Rothenberg is an internationally known poet with over eighty books of poetry and twelve assemblages of traditional and avant-garde poetry such as *Technicians of the Sacred* and *Poems for the Millennium.* His most recent big book is *Eye of Witness: A Jerome Rothenberg Reader,* and he is now working on a global and historical anthology of "outside and subterranean poetry."

Mary Kay Rummel is the first Poet Laureate of Ventura County, CA. Her seventh book of poetry, *The Lifeline Trembles,* has been published by Blue Light Press of San Francisco as a co-winner of the 2014 Blue Light Poetry prize. She teaches part time at California State University, Channel Island and lives in Ventura.

Dixie Salazar has five books of poetry: *Hotel Fresno* , Blue Moon Press, *Reincarnation of the Commonplace* (national poetry award winner), Salmon Run Press, *Blood Mysteries,* Univ. of Arizona and *Flamenco Hips and Red Mud Feet,* Univ. of Arizona Press. *Limbo,* her novel, was published by White Pine press 1995. Her newest collection *Altar for Escaped Voices,* Tebot Bach in 2013. In February 2014, her young adult novel *Carmen and Chia Mix Magic* will be published by Black Opal Books. Website: dixieslazar.com

Benjamin Saltman (d.) began writing poetry in 1965 with his first book published in 1968. Since then, numerous books, poems and awards have come his way. He began teaching writing in 1967 at Cal State Northridge .His influence on so many students, who became friends and poets in their own right is astounding. His books belong on every poet's shelf. From his poem "Shadows" – *But outside in the yard shadows are feathers/piled under the apricot tree. As the sun moves/they slip out of the earth and dry themselves,/and pluck damp grassblades one by one./ They gather huge delicate wings along the wall.*

E.R. Sanchez has had a short story and many poems published. He wrote his first novel, *Remedy: Inspired by Life Experience* due out in 2014.

Trinidad Sanchez, Jr (d.) Trino was recognized for his activism on behalf of those in the penal system and his involvement in peace and justice. He's been featured at numerous venues throughout the country. His essays, literary reviews and poems have been published in several anthologies. Activist/poet, Ricardo Sanchez wrote of Trino's book, *Why Am I So Brown?* It is a song of realization and an outcry which dares to confront the evil perfidy of institutional MAN...and it is a most moving poetics which has no need to be coy, petty, nice, neat not safe...

Terry Sanville lives in San Luis Obispo with his artist-poet wife (his in-house editor) and one freaky cat (his in-house critic). He writes full time, producing short stories, essays, poems an occasional play and novels.His poetry and short stories have been accepted by more than 180 literary and commercial journals and anthologies including the *Picayune Literary Review, Birmingham Arts Journal, Shenandoah,* and the *Boston Literary Magazine.* He was nominated for a Pushcart Prize for his short story "The Sweeper". Terry is a retired urban planner and an accomplished jazz and blues guitarist – who once played with a symphony orchestra backing up jazz legend George Shering.

Steven Sher a Brooklyn native is the author of 14 books including, most recently, *Grazing on Stars: Selected Poems* (Presa Press, 2012) and *The House of Washing Hands* (Pecan Grove Press, 2014) He has taught many workshops and at many universities for more than 35 years. In 2012, he and his wife moved to Jerusalem. Find out more about his writing at stevensher.net

Nancy Shiffrin has 2 poetry collections in print, *The Vast Unknowing,* Infinity Publishing, 2013, bbotw.com and *Game with Variations,* unibook.com. She also writes reviews, scholarly articles and fiction. Her work has appeared in numerous publications nationally and internationally.

Jerry Douglas Smith, 2013 & 2014 Poet Laureate of San Luis Obispo. A Salida, Colorado native, Jerry's been a storyteller all his life. He acquired a natural education informed by rivers, raccoons, Native Americans, smart trout and wise old forests. A backpacker and fly-fisherman, he's a naturalist in the old sense, and insatiably curious student of human nature and the universe.

M.J. Smith has degrees in literature from Northern Arizona University and New York University. He currently teaches literature and composition at the City College of San Francisco. Through his imprint KC Books, he edited and published the collected poems of Ray Clark Dickson, *Parlando*. He was a selected poet at the 1992 SLO Poetry Festival.

K.H. Solomon is a retired agricultural engineer, whose career specialized n water management. He began writing poetry to capture the sounds and smells of foreign markets, the colors and textures of new crops, and the remarkable characters that peopled his agricultural adventures.

Dian Sousa is drinking companion and reverend to the heretical and free. Big Yes Press recently published her third book, *The Marvels Recorded in My Private Closet*. She has been nominated for a Pushcart Prize. Dian was the Poet Laureate for San Luis Obispo in 2008.

Gabriel Spera's second book of poems, *The Rigid Body*, was awarded the 2011 Richard Snyder prize from Ashland Poetry Press. His first book of poems, *The Standing Wave*, was a 2002 National Poetry Series selection and also received the 2004 Literary Book Award from the National Endowment for the Arts and a 2014 COLA grant from the City of Los Angeles. A resident of Los Angeles, he participated in the 18th, 20th and 29th Annual San Luis Obispo Poetry Festivals.

David St. John is the author of ten collections of poetry, most recently, *The Auroras*, published by Harper Collins in 2012. He lives in Venice Beach, California.

Leslie St. John, a native of Little Rock, AR. Is a poet, yogi and expression advocate. She received her MFA from Purdue University and is the author of *Beauty Like a Rope*, Word Palace Press. Her poems appear in various journals, including *Cimarron Review, Crab Orchard Review, Florida Review, Indiana Review Oxford American* and *Verse Daily*. She teaches English at Cuesta and Cal Poly and hosts Prose and Poses, writing and yoga workshops along the Central Coast.

David Starkey served as Santa Barbara's 2009-2010 Poet Laureate and is Director of the Creative Writing Program at Santa Barbara City College. His poetry has appeared in many journals, including *The American Scholar, The Georgia Review* and *The Southern Review*, and in his six full-length collections, most recently *It Must Be Like the World* and *Circus Maximus*.

Lani Steele is a native Californian. She has traveled in over 80 countries and lived in four, including the Philippines and Chad. *A Plague of Angels* was written in several places over many years. This is her second collection. She was included in several anthologies and many literary publications. She has been an educator and continues to work in the field. Steele lives in Los Osos with her husband Gary, she has four children and five grandchildren.

Hannah Stein, who lives in Davis, California, has made many delightful visits to San Luis Obispo, visiting friends and reading her work. Her poems appear widely in journals, among them the *American Poetry Review, Beloit Poetry Journal, Poetry Flash, Prairie Schooner,* and *Yale Review*. Her book, *Earthlight*, La Questa Press and chapbooks *Schools of Flying Fish, Greatest Hits* and *A Broken Music* from State Street, Pudding House and Finishing Line Press.

340

Lisa M. Steinman's most recent books are *Invitation to Poetry* from Wiley-Blackwell and *Absence and Presence* from the University of Tampa Press, 2013. She is a recipient of awards from the National Endowment for the Arts, the Oregon Arts Commission, and the Rockefeller Foundation. She is also co-editor of the poetry magazine *Hubbub* and teaches at Reed College in Portland, Oregon.

Roslyn Strohl was born and educated in Australia and taught school in Australia, England and Chicago before moving to California and settling at a kind of half point in California with the man from Chicago she met in Barcelona. For the last thirty years she has relished working as a psychotherapist. The Language of the Soul, poetry, is her grounding and liberation. Reading and writing poems is all she can manage, so this publication is a gift. The Poetry Festival is a joy.

Kevin Patrick Sullivan's books include, *First Sight, The Space Between Things,* and *Under Such Brilliance.* His poems have appeared in *ASKEW, SOLO, Hummingbird* and other journals in print and on the web, including *Other Voices International.* He was the guest editor for SOLO Café I & II. A past Poet Laureate for the City of San Luis Obispo and Co-Founder/Curator of the Annual San Luis Obispo Poetry Festival and the monthly reading series Corners of the Mouth since 1984. He is also the Founder/Curator of Poetry at the Steynberg and is Co-Organizer of the 100 Thousand Poets/Musicians For Change Events in San Luis Obispo.

Patti Sullivan is the author of two chapbooks, *For the Day,* DeerTree Press 2012 and *Not Fade Away,* Finishing Line Press, 2014. Her poems have appeared in *Askew, ARTLIFE, Solo Novo, Café Solo* and *Hummingbird.* She assists with the Annual San Luis Obispo Poetry Festival & the monthly readings, Corners of the Mouth and Poetry at the Steynberg.

Phil Taggart has three collections of poetry, his newly published *Rick Sings,* Brandenburg Press, *Opium Wars,* Mille Grazie Press and an art book in collaboration with Texas artist Ann Harithas, *Cowboy Collages.* He served for nine years as the Poetry Editor of *Art Life,* and is currently editor/publisher of *Askew* with Marsha de la O and Friday Lubina. He serves his community as a Cultural Affairs Commissioner. He grew up in South Whittier and now lives in Ventura, California, with his wife Marsha de la O.

Rosalee Thompson (d.) "I was a kid that sat in the back of the classroom never answering the teacher's questions because I was busy in my head making up my own. Being unconventional has led me through a lifelong adventure, from singing in nightclubs to acting in theater. My birthday is September 16, Mexican Independence Day, which I consider an omen of my being. It's been quite a celebration. I'm still asking questions but I learned that love is the always answer".

Imani Tolliver is a poet, visual artist and educator. In 2007/2008 she served as Poet Laureate for the Watts Towers Arts Center in L.A. California. She has read all around the country, including the Smithsonian Institute, Beyond Baroque and the L.A. Central Library. Imani volunteers, marches and pitches in whenever she is able, in support of the vibrant and beautiful LGBT community of which she is wholly and happily a part.

Jennifer Tseng's first book, *The Man With My Face,* (AAWW2005), won the Asian American Writer's Workshop National Poetry Manuscript Competition and a 2006 PEN American Center's Open Book Award. Her new book, *Red Flower, White Flower,* Marick Press 2013, winner of the 2012 Marick Press Poetry Prize, features English originals alongside Chinese translations by Mengying Han and Arron Crippen. She works at the West Tisbury Free Public Library on Martha's Vineyard.

James Tyner's awards include the 2008 Coal Hill Review Chapbook contest, the Larry Levis poetry prize, the Ernesto Trejo Poetry Prize and the Andres Montoya Scholarship. His work has appeared in many journals and anthologies and he was recently installed as the first Poet Laureate of Fresno.

Amy Uyematsu is a sansei poet and former high school math teacher from Los Angeles. She has had three published collections: *30 Miles from J-Town, Nights of Fire, Nights of Rain* and *Stone Bow Prayer.*

Patrice Vecchione is a poet, author, editor, teacher and artist. She is excited that her second nonfiction book, *Step into Nature: Nurturing Imagination & Spirit in Everyday Life* will be published by Beyond Words/Atria, an imprint of Simon & Schuster in the spring of 2015. Her most recent collection of poetry is *The Knot Untied.* She's the editor of many anthologies for Penguin Putnam, Henry Holt and Cricket Books. For many years Patrice has taught poetry to children and adults through her program The Heart of the Word: Poetry and Imagination. She is also a collage artist.

Jon Veinberg is the author of 5 poetry collections, the latest, *Angels at Bus Stops,* is forthcoming this year from Lynx House Press. He has been a two time NEA recipient.

Gloria L. Velasquez: Considered an early pioneer of the Chicano Art Renaissance, Gloria is an internationally acclaimed author who holds a Ph.D. from Stanford University in Latin American and Chicano Lit. She is the author of two bi-lingual collections of poetry as well as the Roosevelt High School Series featuring nine novels. The Special Collections at Stanford has honored her with "The Gloria Velasquez Papers" archiving her life as a writer and humanitarian. Gloria was the Poet Laureate for San Luis Obispo in 2006.

Ken Waldman has six full-length poetry collections, a memoir, a children's poetry book and nine CD's that combine Appalachian-style string-band music with original poems. A former college professor, since 1995 he's made his living as a freelance writer, musician, performer and educator, often touring as Alaska's Fiddling poet.

Don Wallis has been writing and reading his poems in public for over fifty years. He is a survivor of riots, skid rows and the sticks and a spokesperson for children, social change and mental health. He is also a prose writer, artist and puppeteer. Learn more at www.arttradition.com.

Viola Weinberg was the first Poet Laureate of Sacramento, California (2000-2002). The author of five poetry books, and the happy recipient of numerous awards, including the Glenna Luschei Distinguished Poet Award. She lives in rural Sonoma County and writes in a yurt. She is currently at work on a collaboration with photographer Peter Spencer titled, *Ghosts of Electricity.*

Jonathan Weinert, author of *Thirteen Small Apostrophies,* Back Pages and *In the Mode of Disappearance,* Nightboat, winner of the Nightboat Poetry Prize. He is co-editor with Kevin Prufer of *Until Everything is Continuous Again: American Poets on the recent Work of W.S. Merwin,* WordFarm, 2012. He is a recipient of an Artist's Fellowship in poetry from the Massachusetts Cultural Council, he lives in Stow, MS, with the poet Amy M. Clark and their son Jonah.

Jackson Wheeler grew up in Southern Appalachia in the town of Andrews, N.C. he attended UNC Chapel Hill on scholarship and has been living in Ventura County, CA and working with intellectually disabled adults since 1975.

Paul J. Willis is a professor of English at Westmont College and a former Poet Laureate of Santa Barbara. His most recent collection is *Say This Prayer into the Past*, Cascade books 2013. You may learn more about him at www.pauljwillis.com

Rosemary Wilvert spends as much time as possible outdoors, gardening, hiking and camping with her husband, Cal. She was Poet Laureate of San Luis Obispo in 2007.

Nellie Wong has published 3 collections of poetry and a chapbook. *Breakfast Lunch Dinner* was published in 2012 by Meridian Press Works. Two of her poems are engraved on public sites in San Francisco, where she lives. Her alma mater, Oakland High School (Oakland, CA) named a building after her in 2011.

J-son Wooi-Chin had this to say: I teach and write poems. Mostly, I want to think of myself as a writer who teaches and who travels to different remote places in this world, looking at how people live, how I might live, and try to make sense of who I am.

Toni Wynn's six – year stay on the Central Coast incubated, then announced her voice, providing bedrock for her writing life. Shakespeare Press Museum, Mille Grazie and Sea Moon presses published keepsake portfolios, books and chapbooks of her work. Toni now writes by the water in Hampton, Virginia. Stop by at toniwynn.com

Ricardo Means Ybarra. Tile setter, surfer, lover of SLO poetry, kidnapped by two wiener dogs, I will continue to write on short streets.

Al Young: Widely translated and acclaimed, Al Young's many books include poetry, *Something About the Blues: An Unlikely Collection of Poetry, Coastal Night and Inland Afternoons: Poems 2001-2006. The Sound of Dreams Remembered: Poems 1990-2000, Heaven: Poems Collected 1956-1990,* fiction, *Seduction by Light, Sitting pretty, Who Is Angelina?* Musical memoirs, *Mingus Mingus: Two Memoirs, Drowning in the Sea of Love, Kinds of Blue, Things Ain't What They Used To Be, Bodies & Soul.* From 2005-2008 he served as Poet Laureate of California. Other honors include NEA, Fulbright and Guggenheim Fellowships. *The Sea, The Sky, And You, And I,* a poetry & jazz CD, featuring bassist Dan Robbins, came out last year from Bardo Digital. He currently teaches at California College of the Arts, San Francisco. Exhaustive information about this Berkeley-based author may be found at www.AlYoung.org

Bonnie Young is one of four authors of the poetry collection *Where Our Palms Rest,* Coalesce Press 2013 and the author of the chapbook, *Inside Pockets,* John Daniel, 2009. Her work has appeared in journals, including *Rattle, The Midwest Quarterly, Flyway, Thema,* and elsewhere. Her poem, *To the God of Light and Shadow,* was chosen by the Canzona Women's Ensemble for a commissioned piece of choral music by Dr. Meredith Brammeir. As SLO Poet Laureate, Young and volunteers shared poetry with over 700 elementary students.

Gary Young's books include *Hands, The Dream of a Moral Life, Days, Braver Deeds and Pleasure.* His book, *No Other Life* won the William Carlos Williams Award, and in 2009 he received the Shelley Memorial Award. His *Even So: New and Selected Poems,* was released last year from White Pine Press.

R. Yurman. Despite 55 years of "Cease and Desist" orders, R. Yurman has gone on committing poetry with little regard for the consequences. Now joined by grandson Jacob, who despite his tender years has become a glutton for language, these co-conspirators sing and glory in the power of words as they dance through their days.

THE ALMOST COMPLETE HISTORY OF THE FEATURED AND SELECTED READERS AT THE ANNUAL SAN LUIS OBISPO POETRY FESTIVAL

Corners of the Mouth

Celebrating

30 years

*Annual S. L. O.
Poetry Festival*

Thanks for going along on this journey with me. It has been quite the adventure, of course when you start things like a poetry festival or a monthly reading series you don't plan ahead other than a few months maybe a year at the most. So you don't save everything or maybe you try to save everything but it just doesn't happen. Things fall through the cracks, or just disappear. I've moved four times during that 30 years, had a number of girlfriends and of course met my wife, Patti, at the 15th ANNUAL SAN LUIS OBISPO POETRY FESTIVAL.

Life presents opportunities to lose things and I lost things.

The 4th ANNUAL SLO POETRY FESTIVAL posters and flyers are gone. I know I missed a number of selected readers who came from all over the state, really the Southwest on their own dime to read for 8 to 10 minutes on a bill that featured some of the best contemporary poets from across America. I'm sorry your name is not here. I am what I am and I am thankful.

Thankful for your patience and understanding, thankful for your generous efforts to come here to San Luis Obispo, Ca. and enrich not just my life but the life of my community.

Which brings us back to the title Corners of the Mouth, a hexagram from the, *I Ching* Hexagram 27, nourishment in to the body from the mouth and nourishment out from the mouth into the community's body. Thank you all the poets, all the audience members, all the community organizations and businesses, thank you for enriching all our lives.

Kevin Patrick Sullivan
Co-Founder/ Curator/Editor

#1. 1984

Ron Bast
Gordon Curzon
Kevin Patrick Sullivan
Karl Kempton
Bill McCollum
Bruce Badrigian
Michael Churchman
Jimmy Kennedy
Torre Houlgate-West
Chuck Paul
Vickie Kelly
Norman Hammond
Pat Manyak
Jan Dove
Glenna Luschei
Edith Cook
San Dei English
Susanne Freeborn
Don Wallis & His Puppets
Music by Terry Sanville

#2. 1985
Nettie Rosburg
Lucille Janisse
Marguerite Costigan
Michael Churchman
Randall A. Ruff
Torre Houlgate-West
Bruce David Badrigian
Norman Hammond
Chuck Paul
Ingrid Reti
Christine Neilson
R.M.Russell
Kevin Patrick Sullivan
Frankie Nemko
San Dei English
Richard Krejsa
Stan Williams
Susan Phelan
Dorothy Siegel
Lani Steele
Jane Elsdon
Vickie Kelly
Mark McCormick
Sheirleen Branden
Peter Kittel (Prose)
Jim Cushing
Karl Kempton
Dian Sousa
Glenna Luschei
Don Wallis & His Puppets
Music by Terry Sanville &
Norman Hammond

#3. 1986

Ed Martin
James Cushing
Ingrid Reti
Lucille Janisse
Randy Ruff
Edwin Shaw
S Reichman
Peter Kittel
Kevin Patrick Sullivan
Elizabeth Jianuzzi
Cezanne Rivers
Don Rosburg
John Franklin
Gordon Curzon
Jean Marie Dancer
Jane Elsdon
Marguerite Costigan
Vickie Kelly
William Little
Paul Portugés
Christine Neilson
Music – Terry Sanville
James Houlihan
Music Norman Hammond
R.M. Russel
Music Ken McCool
Carol Lee Sanchez
Vasco Sena
Michael Churchman
San Dei English
Doris Collins
Gary McSwane
Cappy Paul
Abd al hay Moore
Stuart Presley
T.N. Moreno
Michael May

Norm Hammond
Phyllis Davies
Marion Wolfe
Teresa L. McKinley
Karl Kempton
Craig Andrews
Mark McCormick
Glenna Luschei
Nettie Rosburg
Terry Sanville
L.Lee Davis
Jimmy Kennedy

(#4. 1987 is missing)

#5. 1988

Ricardo Means Ybarra
Melissa Rissman
Chuck Paul
Marguerite Costigan
Karl Kempton
James Leddy
Vickie Kelly
Margaret Nadey
R. David Colby
Margaret C. Lange
Cynthia Anderson
James Cushing
Betty Weitnenkamp
Sonja Hannon
Edie Lewis
Kevin Patrick Sullivan
Norman Hammond
S. Reichman
John Manning
J.K. Mountain
Harriet Kofalk
Ingrid Reti
Music by Terry Sanville
Music by Tony Brown

#6. 1989

Gordon Curzon
Jane Elsdon
Pleasant Gehman
Lauran Hoffman
Priscilla Piche
P.R. Dubois
Harriet Kofalk
Phyllis Davies
Ryn Wood
George Nowell
L.N. Buffett
Pam Reichman
Scott Jenkins
Carne Logren
Laura Evans
J.K. Mountain
Marguerite Costigan
Kevin Patrick Sullivan
Ingrid Reti
Norman Hammond
Ed Martin
Marion Wolfe
Karl Kempton
Maía
Marsha de la O

7. 1990

Chuck Paul
Susan Balkman
Jay Bonestell
Richard Kresja
Margaret Nadey
Becca Carmona
Marlene Pearson
Paula Harvey
Kurt Doerfler
Angy Bjorkuln
John Manning
Katie Lindsay
P.M. Piche
Donna Page
Scott Bird
Steve Canada
Shelba Robison
Ray Forman
Marguerite Costigan
Norman Hammond
Joseph Gallo
Kate Gale Harper
Maía
Nick Campbell
Ben Saltman
Judy Graham
Selene Cohen
Hernán Castellano-Girón
J-son Wooi-chin
Ricardo Means Ybarra
Melissa Rissman
Sylvia Reichman
Music by Norman Hammond
and Terry Sanville

#8. 1991

Mike Newell
Ron Harris
Mary Parker
Tomas Renault
Lee Davis
Paul Angeloni
Ruth Hoffman-Mortola
Kirsten Wohl
Ray Forman
Ed Martin
Ingrid Reti
Don Wallis
Nicholas Campbell
Marguerite Costigan
Norman Hammond - Music
Sojourner Kincaid-Rolle
Ben Saltman
Joseph Gallo
Hernán Castellano-Girón
Kevin Patrick Sullivan
Michael McLaughlin
Abigail Albrecht
Ray Clark Dickson
J-son Wooi-chin
Maía
Cynthia Anderson

#9. 1992

Jasmine Marshall
Cynthia Anderson
Trudy Wischermann
Laurel Ann Bogen
Ben Saltman
Jackson Wheeler
Mitch Smith
Hernán Castellano-Girón
Steve Word
Ray Clark Dickson
Shelba Cole Robison
Merilene M. Murphy
Connie Richmond
Michael McLaughlin
Nicholas Campbell
Audrey Johnson
Don Wallis
Sylvia Reichman
Rik Thorensen
Steven White
Torre Houlgate-West
Jane Elsdon
Andrew Susac
Susan Hecht
Crystal Word
Marion Wolfe
Joseph Gallo
J. Ellsworth Weaver
Maía
Steve C. Kaplan
Abigail Albrecht
Lani Steele
Renee Everett
Roslyn Strohl
David Oliveira
Richard Leddy
Judy Graham

Keith Denny
Rich Mealy
Suebob Davis
Terri B. Joseph
Kate Gale Harper
Ricardo Means Ybarra
Al Leddy
J-son Wooi-chin
Amanda Swamy
Iva M. Rayburn
Kevin Patrick Sullivan
Sojourner Kincaid-Rolle
Jim Leddy
Terry Kennedy

#10. 1993
Featured Readers:
Benjamin Saltman
Kate Gale Harper
Michael Hannon
Anita Wilkins
Karl Kempton
Glenna Luschei
Kevin Patrick Sullivan
Christine Meyer
Nicholas Campbell
David Oliveira
Marguerite Costigan
Scheduled Readers:
Andrew Susac
Barbara Ehrenstrom
Francesca Nemko
Robert Simola
Abigail Albrecht
Cynthia Anderson
Michael McLaughlin
Mary Exline
Lisa Belile
P.M. Piche
Sojourner Kincaid-Rolle
Kristen Drolshagen
E. Lincoln
Dwight Johnson
Mary Morris
Velva Maguire Hakim
Angy Bjorklund
Shanin M. Green
Joseph Gallo
Gerry Marr
Eric Priestly
Lee Duke

Dian Sousa
Francis M. Svedas
Russ Hileman
Melissa Rissman
David Ciaffardini
Marni Grant
J. Ellsworth Weaver
Ward R. Spencer
Suebob Davis
Rik Thorensen
Victoria Fox
Crystal Dickerson
Steve Canada
David Ciaffardini
Marion Wolfe
Angy Bjorklund
Sylvia Howell Kneller
Margaret C. Lange
Brent Cunningham
Debbie Dominguez
Jordon Jones
Shelba Robison
Jim Schrotel
Criss Cannady
Don Wallis

#11. 1994

Featured Readers:

Will Inman
Jackson Wheeler
Merilene M. Murphy
Dian Sousa
Ray Clark Dickson
Kathy Fagan
Angie Estes
Kevin Clark
Rosalee
Don Wallis

Selected Readers:

Shelba Robison
Justin Pheley
Terri Joseph
David Oliveira
Christine Becher
Carmen V. Fojo
Toni Wynn
Francee Rios
Kevin Patrick Sullivan
Margaret C. Lange
Anne G. Phillips
John Souza
Marsha Evans
Lani Steele
Michael McLaughlin
Torre Houlgate-West
Lily Marie Livingston
Criss Cannady
Sojourner K. Rolle
Will Jones
Valentina Gnup-Krup
Wendy Lawton
Joseph Gallo
Abigail Albrecht
Barbara Morningstar

Stan Williams
Hunter Lillis
Nancy Abbott
Edith Cook
Elenor Ehrenstrom
Steve Word
Mary Schiller
David Ciaffardini
Thomas A Brill
Camini Tripodi

#12. 1995
Featured Readers:
Terry Sanville
Don Wright
Marsha de la O
Amy Uyematsu
Jayne McPherson
Lance Lee
Carol Muske
James Cushing
Joan M. Raymond
Torre Houlgate-West
Ginger Adcock
Selected Readers:
Marguerite Costigan
Mike Carlin
Laura Golden Bellotti
Mary McCarthy
Beth Ann Bronkey
James Rossignol
Mud Baron
Carla Martinez
Cathy A. Coleman
Roger Aplon
Phil Taggart
Judith Taylor
Rich Yurman
Mark Magiera
Lee McCarthy
Dianna Henning
Mark Haile
Laurie Suzanne Lessen
Joseph Milosch
Lucia Casalinuovo
Marni L. Parker
Cathleen Long
Elnora McNoughton
Dona Loungo Stein

#13. 1996
Featured Readers:
Naomi Lazard
Peter Gizzi
Valentina Gnup-Krup
Donna Loungo Stein
Roger Aplon
Corrine Ardoin
Rosemary Wilvert
Anne G.Phillips
Gwendolyn Alley
Stan Williams
Toni Wynn
Denis Johnson
Frances Mayes
Gary Thompson
Cecile Pineda
and selected readers

#14. 1997
Featured Readers:
Paul Zimmer
Kevin Clark
Shelba Cole Robison
Toni Kathleen Flynn
Michael McLaughlin
Margaret C. Lange
Carla Martinez
Beth Ann Bronkey
Margaret Gardner
Ivan Simon
John Franklin
Edward Field
(selected readers)
Childrens Poetry Workshop
w/Christine Becher

#15. 1998
Featured Readers:
Stanley Plumly
Angie Estes
Ray Clark Dickson
Hannah Stein
Michael Hannon
Karl Kempton
Anne G. Phillips
Ray Forman
Kyoko A. Partin
Anne Candelaria
Brenda Nasio
Jerry Douglas Smith
The Jimm Cushing Paradox
Dian Sousa
Kevin Patrick Sullivan
Rachel Kann
David Oliveira
Christine Becher
and selected readers

#16. 1999
Featured Readers:
Eavan Boland
Siobhan Campbell
Glenna Luschei
Gary Young
Steve Kowit
Enid Osborn
Eldra Avery
Lois Klein
Rosemary Wilvert
Paul Willis
Sean Raymond
Scott Nairen
Phil Taggart
Gloria L. Velasquez
Lorna Dee Cervantes
Merilene M. Murphy
Minerva & C.P.I.T.S students
Hernán Castellano-Girón
Zaffi Gousopoulos
Selected Readers:
Gail H. Clark
Annee Garrett
Amy Frances
C. Chad Hoffman
Kyoko Asano Partin
Amber West
Tom Law
Michelle Margolis
Tom Marshall
Yvonne Postelle
Anne Candelaria

#17. 2000
Featured Readers:
Rodney Jones
Jim Natal
Jeanette M. Clough
Christopher Buckley
Rich Yurman
Sara Backer
Dian Sousa
SLO H.S. Lit. Club
Marguerite Costigan
Don Wallis
Ray Clark Dickson
Glenna Luschei
Hernán Castellano-Girón
Carolyn Kizer
Jackson Wheeler
Trinidad Sanchez, Jr.
Suzanne Lummis
Selected Readers:
Pete Justus
Jack Shafer
Gail H. Clark
Sylvia Alcon
Briana Urzana
Mehnaz Sahibzada
Valentina Gnup
Marcus Kugler
Brian Bywater
Consuelo Underwood
Stuart Presley
Carmen Rose
Ira White
Deborah Tobola
Rebecca Martin
Barbara Marysdaughter

#18. 2001
Featured Readers:
Nellie Wong
Sandra M. Gilbert
Gail H. Clark
David Dominguez
James Cushing
Karl Kempton
Larry Jaffe
Anne Candelaria
Linda Bierds
Jon Veinberg
Dixie Salazar
Past Poets Laureate & winners
of the SLO County Arts
Council contest
"Perspectives about Places:
Voices from SLO County
Selected Readers:
Patti Sirens
Edward Jamieson, Jr.
Marnie L. Parker
Richard Thielo
Gabriel Spera
Roberta Sherry
Rosemary Scott-Fishburn
Beverly Acuff Momoi
George Tolbert
C.R. Mannering
Ingrid Reti
Eleanor Watson-Gove
Jim Watson-Gove
Cindy L. Pitz
Amy MacLennan
Don Nash
Consuelo Underwood
Jasmeen Miah

#19. 2002
Featured Readers:
Paul Flores
Pat Payne
Steven Sher
Dorothy Barresi
Adrianne Marcus
Ken Waldman
Bob Hicok
Anne Candelaria
Kevin Patrick Sullivan
David Starkey with Plastic
Zipper
Selected Readers:
Michael McLaughlin
Malcolm Julke
Wes Gullidge
Suzanne Jill Levine
Tom Law
Deborah Toboloa
Jerry Douglas Smith
David Ochs
Jane Elsdon
Deborah Paes de Barros
Kimi Julian
Rosemary Wilvert

#20. 2003
Featured Readers:
Michael McLaughlin
Jane Elsdon
Rosemary Wilvert
Lisa M. Steinman
Dian Sousa
James Cushing
Jack Foley
Adelle Foley
Richard Silberg
Joyce Jenkins
Kevin Patrick Sullivan
Kevin Clark
Ray Clark Dickson
Jerry Douglas Smith
Marguerite Costigan
Margaret C. Lange
Karl Kempton
Jacqueline Marcus
Glenna Luschei
B.H. Fairchild
Don Wallis
Tom Law
Anne Candelaria
Gabriel Spera
Rachel Kann
Criss E. Cannady
David Ochs
Michael Hannon
Hernán Castellano-Girón
Selected Readers:
Wanda Snow Porter
Michael J. O'Brien
Tiffany Fabricius
Dawn McGuire
Catherine Ruffing
Amy MacLennan

Betty Edmundson
Consuelo Marshall
Wes Guillidge
Music from Terry Sanville &
Norman Hammond

#21. 2004
Featured Readers:
Michael McLaughlin
Jane Elsdon
Mark Fabionar
Imani Tolliver
Pedro Arroyo
Kyoko Asano
Sonia Paz Baron-Vine
Peter Everwine
C.G. Hanzlicek
Michael Datcher
Selected Readers:
Theresa Mortilla
Susan Hoffman
Evelyn Cole
Nan Cohen
R.N. Homer Christensen
Wendy Jeanne Burch
Rudy Flores
Matt Godde
Danielle Osborne
Katey Maruska
Anne Knowles
Larry Greco Harris
Angela Hoxsey
Francesca Nemko
with bassist Ken Husted

22. 2005

Featured Readers:
Anne Candelaria
Ray Clark Dickson
Michael McLaughlin
Hernán Castellano-Girón
Jane Elsdon
Gloria L, Velasquez
Christopher Buckley
Glenna Luschei
Al Young
Kevin Patrick Sullivan
Dian Sousa
Selected Readers:
Marguerite Costigan
Dan J. Curtis
Ruth Goodnow
Irman Arcibal
Dori Marier
Joseph Geever
Teri Patterson
Ken Solomon
Don Wallis
Roy K. Johnston
David Ochs
Sylvia Alcon

#23. 2006
Featured Readers:
Gloria L Velasquez
Rosemary Wilvert
Roy K. Johnston
Jacqueline Marcus
Gail H. Clark
Lisa Coffman
Rudy Calderon
Donald Revell
James Cushing
Jaki Shelton Green
Michele Flom
Michael C. Ford
Landis Everson
Selected Readers:
Nixson Borah
Jasmine Marshall Armstrong
George Burns
Tamara Madison
Linda Camplese
Edward T. Martin
Gail H. Clark
Philip Valle
Michaelann Dimitrijevich
Ben Simon
Scott Barrett
Doren Robbins

#24. 2007
Featured Readers:
Rosemary Wilvert
Dian Sousa
Kevin Clark
Hernán Castellano-Girón
Michael Hannon
Phoebe McAdams
David. St. John
Nixson Borah
Jackson Wheeler
Andrea Selch
Leo Victor Briones
Indigo Moor
Dan Gerber
Selected Readers:
Maggie Webbey
Don Wallis
Avra Kouffman
David Kann
Ursula Black
Tim Pompey
Bruce Henderson
Edward T. Martin

25. 2008
Featured Readers:
Dian Sousa
James Cushing
Kate Gale
Ray Clark Dickson
Denise Duhamel
Glenna Luschei
Viola Weinberg
Kevin Patrick Sullivan
Anne Candelaria
The Plein Air Poets of SLO:
Marguerite Costigan
Jane Elsdon
Rosemary Wilvert
Cal Wilvert
Paula C. Lowe
Sylvia Alcon
Selected Readers:
Lani Steele
Roslyn Strohl
Michaelann Dimitrijevich
Ivan BrownOtter

 # 26. 2009
Featured Readers:
James Cushing
Ray Clark Dickson
Michael C. Ford
Sharon Dougiago
Sally Ashton
Michael Hannon
Hannah Stein
Lee Herrick
Jennifer Tseng
James Tyner
Paul Fericano
Selected Readers:
Bonnie Young
Ellyn Winslow
Lisa Coffman
Amber Cloverdale Sumrall
Paula C. Lowe
Don Wallis

27. 2010
Featured Readers:
Eleanor Lerman
Paul Lobo Portugés
Kevin Clark
Sarah Murphy
Gregory Ramirez
Bill Pearlman
Amy M. Clark
Bonnie Young
Anne Candelaria
Glenna Luschei
Ricardo Means Ybarra
J-son Wooi-chin
Luke Warm Water
SOLO Press Poets:
Barry Spacks- Perie Longo –
George Burns
Selected Readers:
Ken Solomon
Tamara Madison
Russell Read
Jonathan Weinert
David Starkey
Brooklyn Rose

28. 2011
Featured Readers:
Clayton Eshleman
Glenna Luschei
Bonnie Young
Ray Clark Dickson
Jacqueline Berger
Christopher Buckley
Rosemary Wilvert
Samuel Hiram Duarte
Jerry Douglas Smith
Harry E. Northup
Lisa Coffman
SOLO Novo Poets:
M. Frias-May
Lisa McCool
Selected Readers:
Benjamin Daniel Lawless
Beverly A. Boyd
Tamara Madison
Leslie St. John

#29. 2012
Featured Readers:
Tamara Madison
Joel Katz
Bonnie Young
Jerry Douglas Smith
Leslie St. John
Michael Hannon
Dixie Salazar
Paul Lobo Portugés
Sam Hamill
Suzanne Roberts
Sam Pereira
Gabriel Spera
Selected Readers:
Jeanie Greensfelder
Michael McLaughlin
Anne Candelaria
Patti Sullivan
David Kann
Rob Seitz
James Cushing

#30. 2013
Featured Readers:
"The Signature of all Things"
A film on the Occasion of the
100th
Anniversary of Kenneth
Rexroth's Birth.
Filmed at Beyond Baroque and
introduced by M.C. Ford.

Mary Kay Rummell
Nixson Borah
Michael Hannon
Sylvia Alcon
Marguerite Costigan
Patrice Vecchione
Jerry Douglas Smith
Klipschutz
Glenna Luschei
Jerome Rothenberg
Lee Rossi
Rosemary Wilvert
Robert Krut
Paula C. Lowe
Selected Readers:
Will Jones
Linda Camplese
Nancy Shiffrin
Victoria Billings
Stuart Presley
Mikl Paul
Music from Terry Sanville